12 Days in Nepal

From Bangor to Bagmati

GW00382725

Roy Uprichard

Published by 12 Days Publishing

Copyright © Roy Uprichard

ISBN   978 0 9567092 0 2

Lots of thanks to Liz Baird's Home Group in Bangor Parish for encouragement re the trip, and then support with rehabilitation. Thanks also to Nathanael McMillan for cover design.

Mention must be made of the sterling proof reading team (aka victims): Philip and Deborah McMillan, Philip Ramsey, Andrew Frame and Lynda Barr. Any remaining errors and all bad taste remain through wilful obstinacy, so all angry letters to me at Her Majesty's displeasure, Scrabo Tower

Finally, thank you to all those who were such a privilege to meet, who were so generous with their time and have allowed me to pass on just a little something of their story.

Roy

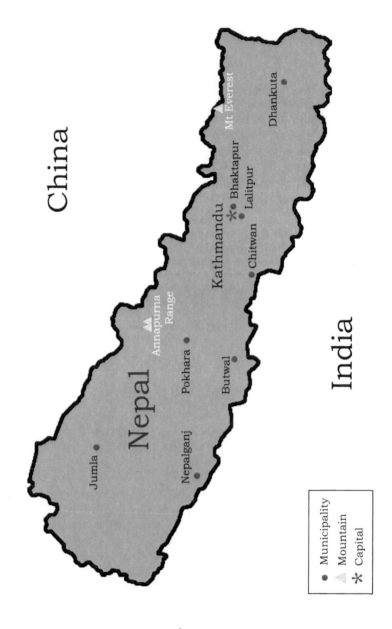

China

India

Nepal

Kathmandu

Annapurna Range

Jumla

Nepalganj

Pokhara

Butwal

Chitwan

Lalitpur

Bhaktapur

Mt Everest

Dhankuta

● Municipality
◢ Mountain
✳ Capital

4

Contents:

5

Day 6

(1)Sun Up and Down Dale/ Mountain Morning / Aussies/ Retreat/Royal Ulster Fry/ Lengthening the stride/ Nayapul/ Taxi?

(2) Bag Ladies/ Tiffin/ Lakeside and Van the Man

Day 7

Exiles/ Airwaves and Carpenters footsteps in the bus park/ Keith Smith/ Paulas Panday/ Chunman and the Street Kids/ The Roof Garden

Day 8

The Egret's shrill/ Jacob Zuma/ Returning Road/ Jam / KISC/ Americana/ Electricity and Water/ Tom Hanks / Mosquito Squadron

Day 9

Some Very Central Points: Information about the range and extent of what FONIC does on the ground./ Skype Home/ Lost/ Globalisation

Day 10

From a Whisper to a Shout/ The March/ Preme La/ Eileen Lodge/ Durbar Square/ The Monarchy/ Grace Rescue Home/ Little Ulsterisms

Day 11

Business as Mission: Top of the World/ Beauty for Ashes/ Faithworks/ Abraham Khan/ Higher Ground and Culture Mix.

6

Introduction:

Ok, the confession! In the final year of my degree at Queen's, I sat modules on the Sociology of Development and Third World Politics. I was interested in these things, you see. I had, of course, already made a contribution to third world debt relief by buying the Band Aid single and staying up late to watch Live Aid and twenty years later, Live 8. I never wanted to actually visit the Third World, until late 2009 when I booked a flight to Kathmandu. How can one account for such a radical turnaround?

The explanation is as follows: My friends, Philip and Deborah McMillan, along with their three children had been in Nepal since 2000, involved in church related development work, and had set up a charity in 2005, FONIC Trust (**F**riends **O**f **N**epali **C**hristians) to work closely with local churches in supporting and resourcing a range of medical, educational, community and children's projects. They had regularly asked me to come out and visit. I had nodded my head politely, but thought 'no way', rationalising it by sagely musing to myself that I couldn't justify the expense...and it would be better to send them the equivalent of the ticket money to help the cause. Of course I never did! No one ever does! This was a successful strategy of avoidance until, in July 2009, I was mugged by a Jackie Pullinger talk. She had worked with heroin addicts in Hong Kong since the mid 1960's and railed against the complacency of the rich west in failing to serve those without our comfortable advantages. I then felt I had to go soon and see for myself what the Third World was actually like! It was all really unfair!

So, this is an idiot guide to Nepal, a diary of a 12 day visit and the mission, should I choose to accept it, was to take place during the Easter holidays of 2010 where I would stumble round parts of Nepal, trying to cause as little damage as possible and avoid self destructing. This is a true account of those 12 days (allowing a day or so either side for travelling), I being of worried mind.

I had hoped to do a bit of trekking close to the Annapurnas, visit some of the projects FONIC are involved in and the small businesses they're associated with. It was also going to be interesting to see how a soft westerner would cope, being exposed to a third world country for the first time and to compare blood pressure, heart rate and cultural shock reactions to when back home. No pool lounging allowed! Unfortunately Philip took me seriously and came up with the possible schedule of:

Arrival and travel to Pokhara

Undertake a 4 day trek in the Annapurnas

Visit Women's Bag Co-op/ Green Pastures/ Distillation plant,

Return to Kathmandu and partake in Easter celebrations

Visit Grace Rescue Home/Orphanage and Mahema industries

Visit local small business such as, Faith Works, Higher Ground Enterprises, Beauty for Ashes Jewellery, Top of the World Coffee,

Local NGO's such as HDCS and ABBS special educational needs project

Finally…Kilroy's Irish Restaurant and then fly home, to get some sleep!!

The only thing missing was the Tractor Factory. Sorry, wrong country!

But even so, this could count as cruel and unusual treatment!

So, let's think about a country that has come out of prolonged violent armed conflict, with an unstable peace process, no centre ground in politics, deeply opposed political visions for the future, forced to work together to agree a reframed shared future. I know it sounds like

Northern Ireland, but we're talking about Nepal here. Of course in some respects, we could have twinning potential, but we'd need to factor in:

Their population of 28 million

Major electricity and water supply issues

Perhaps 70,000 internally displaced people, joining the 130,000; refugees from Bhutan and Tibet

A 50% illiteracy rate

48% unemployed

26 political parties

$25 per week average income

14% inflation rate,

9 major ethnic groups

6 serious infectious diseases

A couple of turtle doves but no partridge in a pear tree, as they don't do Christmas in what was, until recently, the only official Hindu state in the whole world. So it's not all bad!

(Source: CIA World Factbook)

Whilst political instability hampers much needed foreign investment into this technologically backward, landlocked country, things are helped even less by its most recent dubious honour, that of being labelled the most corrupt country in Southern Asia by a Transparency International report (TI), 143rd out of 180. You'd think the Nepalis could have avoided the corruption tag with a few ex gratia contributions to TI members here and there (add lack of initiative to the debit list above)! We only had Robinsongate to try and make a dent with, but got nil points.

Their situation kind of makes Northern Ireland's troubles seem rather tame by comparison. So, armed with a little research, a Lonely Planet guide and a couple of views of episode 3 of Michael Palin's

Himalaya, I strode forth presumptuously, Stanley like, in search of a Doctor. He stroked his chin, offered counselling (politely declined), then looked at the wall chart of regional infectious risk and injected against Hepatitis, Typhoid, Tetanus, Diphtheria and Polio but not Rabies. Kathmandu dogs must be tourist friendly now! Reeling slightly, I decided to make up for that by exiting into a biting February evening in search of a flight. I had to make do with Fight Night on Sky instead!

Day 1

Journeys/ Cultural Shock Troopers/
An Alternative Highway Code.

I had begun this journey the previous evening with a delayed 5:00 pm flight out of Belfast City, arriving on the Heathrow tarmac at 7:00pm, only ten minutes after the gate was supposed to shut for the flight to Doha! Made it anyway and let's fast forward to the departure area for the final 4 hour jump to Kathmandu.

The gate area (in Qatar International Airport) was full of eager intense faces and a variety of back packing fitness trekkers, differing from the more obviously stylised en route to the capital of Qatar. The door opened and we were hit by a shock of heat, smell, light and noise, setting off the rapid fire speech patterns of returning Nepalis that would defy any rapper; the cultural shock troopers assault on the senses. The opening door also stirred some western dreadlocks and very soon the first bus drew away, glancing back in pity at those left in waiting. Ascending the narrow swaying gangway, the small gap between boarding ramp and aircraft was my transition point of no return between our numbered worlds.

I'm in the first wave but the baggage holds seemed full already, a testimony to these serious travellers. A flight attendant struggled with the biggest piece of back packed hand luggage I'd ever seen. It looked more like 17kg than 7 kg. He eventually gave up the unequal

11

struggle and stored it on a seat. The creaking started, then a hint of movement. No packaged deals here, or at least no regularised ones. Beautiful designer tee shirted 10 year old and mother sit across from us rather more crumpled specimens. There's tenderness in touch here between the couples, while the drift of middle England tones intertwine with German, Dutch and Spanish voices. These are UN families of North Face trekkers, whose affluence is masked but expressed in a different way, firstly by the very fact of seats on this plane and then by the quality of designer glasses - travellers all, searching or re-connecting with the mystique and the grandeur of this Himalayan retreat from modernity; country of Ghurkhas, hills, mountains, fierce, tribal, friendly, riven by conflict but held together by what?

We arrive at 6pm local time and it takes an hour to get a Visa sorted out. Approaching the exit point, Jessica (Philip and Deborah's youngest daughter) has talked her way through security to give me my initial greeting and usher safely onwards. I walk out into the descending reddened sun, the mist of haze and dust hanging over a bustling massive car park set from Slumdog Millionaire and Philip and Deborah, there to meet and greet. "What about ya? Thought I'd drop in for a cuppa tea!"

All sorts of thoughts had rustled through my head prior to the trip....that I'd be imposing or they'd be busy and would have to change their schedule etc. This was all nonsense as for them to see someone walk out of the terminal building means a little slice of home, transported and encouraging, reminding them that they're thought about and they're worth getting on a plane to visit. Some thought it would be "the trip of a lifetime." To them it seemed so far away, this mystical heart of Asia, but it was only 10 hours flying time, half of that to Australia and 3 more than to the States. It's not that far you know! It was further on the way back though!

I climb gratefully into a 1984 battered but mean Isuzu Trooper and exit onto the ring road which will lead to their flat and face the first (literally) gripping encounter with the unique local traffic control system. The fact is there is none, apart from survival of the biggest. Roads merge without markings and roundabout protocols are those of a free for all. The blare of the car and motorbike horns rises; three and four squeeze onto small motorbikes, drivers the only ones with helmets on and Sari'd passengers, side saddled with children wedged between. One even had a child on the handlebars.

Crawling at 2 mph, we negotiate the swarm and then, picking up speed to escape from the immediate assault to the senses, we move on to what seemed like the set of a building site movie, then on past hundreds of small shops and small yards with brick piles. You can get welding repairs right next to toilet sellers, tyre shops, newsagents' kiosks, vegetable carts and live and plucked chickens. They all vie for attention with dozens of Chinese three wheeled tractors loading and supplying this swarming hive of activity. Philip drives with clutch, brake, horn and swerve, eventually exiting down a narrow lane. It must be a shortcut to somewhere more open plan. On past lounging stares and kiosks, to a shopping corner with awnings and yawnings and past the outdoor table tennis competition surrounded by enthused lads. Their net's a row of narrow bricks on their side. A sign shouts "Photo Shop Concern"....(I'm beginning to feel a little concerned myself!) and onto an even narrower lane where the ruts and ramps stretch the suspension even further before we suddenly turn through swing gates into a yard outside a three storey building. It was indeed a short cut.....to their house!

We discard shoes at the entrance and enter their middle floor three bedroomed flat a little on the wrong side of the tracks. I throw my bag into the bedroom. The nets shield me from the family seemingly a few feet away on the roof top opposite, bringing in clothes, chatting, playing and just hanging out. I now feel the panic rising and indeed, wonder in a silent scream, "What have I done?" Of course the application of increased medication should bring the panic levels down and help one settle in for a night of noise but nevertheless, I ask when things will start to quieten down. I'm told it settles pretty soon after dark. It doesn't seem possible, but when dusk settles and

13

without street lights, this full throttle city quietens in sync with the approaching night. People retire quickly to the safety of their homes, with the 12 hour power cuts often reinforcing this dawn to dusk activity mode, apart from the tourist hotspots of Thamel, but that's a different story! The embedded cultural wisdom here is that "only bad people go out after dark." That may or may not be true, but I decide not to test the hypothesis out just yet!

The rapidly spreading blanket of quiet is punctuated only by the news hounds barking, bringing the canine population up to speed with who's up or down on the celebrity dog list. It's time at last to unpack the straining bags with presents from family and sweeties and bits from me. Well, I had to lighten the load for a quick getaway if necessary! The chocolate haul is short term bad news for those who are off it for Lent. Easter Sunday is still nine painful days away!

Coffee, pasta and chicken all help to settle the nerves a little. I do notice with interest though, the large bolts and thick padlocks waiting to be applied to the doors. Bedtime's then an uneasy drift into sleep, after 24 hours in transit. Tomorrow, we'll head down to Grace Church (Saturday is their Sunday here in a six day working week) and then it's off to the west for an all day drive to Pokhara, where the trick or trekking will really begin.

Day 2

The Road Well Travelled/ Grace Church/ The view from the flat/ Death Road/ Pokhara/ Sacred Valley / Moondancing

The walk to Grace Church takes 15 minutes through dusty clay and stone paths, negotiating fields with building site sub plots. On through Grace Academy and into a block and tin roof building where there are women in saris on the left, men on the right. No room for

14

cross dressing here! The service runs from 8:30 to about 11:00, depending on the moment or the preacher. We arrive at about 8:45, near the end of their extended worship and sit cross legged on the carpet. The electricity gives up half way through and I realise it's better when the roof fans are on. A mercifully short sermon occurs with lots of repetition; be holy...avoid idols! Back home it's cars and stuff but here it's all that plus the literal. Every street corner seems to have a Hindu shrine. Be attentive to serve God...deal with the evils inside, he says directly to me.

Intense, heartfelt young people mill about in a mix of neat plain shirts and occasional football tops. These are mostly lower caste converts, given opportunity and pathway to dignity as a matter of right, the right to be recognised and affirmed as an individual of value and then empowered to be all they can be, refusing and then discarding the life description they'd been handed by the caste position they were born into. It's been replaced with an allegiance to a new King who grants freedom for prisoners, comfort instead of fatalistic mourning over one's lot and beauty for ashes. Wilberforce would approve, though Brahmins might struggle here.

The walk back uphill leaves me breathless. We are 1300m above sea level here and of course, that's the key factor, not the fact that I just may be slightly overweight or unfit! I repack the necessities for what will be nearly a week away from the flat. While waiting to load up, there's just enough time to take in more of the surrounding view.

The field just opposite their flat contains an uncultivated plot and a pile of cow dung, supplied by the cows kept in the byre adjoining the downstairs space of one of the families in the three storey multiple occupancy house on the right of the plot. It's another little earner here, along with chickens and a goat; everyone seems to have chickens here. Dozens of extra large pizza sized flattened plates of cow dung mix are drying out, stuck to available external walls; this is the main cooking fuel, along with wood, for the 40% of residents who do not have access to the spasmodic electricity. Their cute two year

15

old girl waves at these foreign faces while a lady collects a backpack full of dung from the topped up pile. On the little first floor terrace space, a woman squats and incants to the still rising sun, ushering worship via an Aladdin's lamp with a little flame, instead of genie, emerging from the spout.

The population of Kathmandu is nearly 2 million and growing at 6.5% per year. As a consequence, it's also experiencing a house price boom, but the rural poor still flock to seek their fortune in the tourist, carpet or textile industries, feeding a demand over any sort of organised supply. They're certainly not drawn by the bright lights! A quarter of a mile away, many squat in riverside shacks, with the women constant prey to trafficking or involvement in very basic service industries.

It's time to pile into the Isuzu Trooper for the 220 Km trip west to Pokhara, whilst brightly coloured women in reds and greens wander by in the rising heat mist. Pokhara will be our trekkers' jumping off point, without a safety net. Out onto the ring road and time to conform to the protocol of the car horn, which during the whole trip, ironically brings little evidence of road rage. It doesn't seem to bother the cow sitting unconcerned in the middle of the two lane traffic though! Deborah prays for a safe journey. I nod politely.

Only one proper near death experience occurs. An oncoming lorry with no turbo is attempting to overtake a bus on an incline as we round a corner and faces turn a Whiter Shade of Pale. Philip manages to apply the brakes to the floor...in fact through the floor... but the parachute release and explosive grappling irons bring us to a complete stop just in time, allowing the oncoming lorry to nip back into lane.

This great ranging twisting road winds down over 3,600 feet to the valley floor, the main supply route to Kathmandu from the west and therefore from India. It brings not only trade but Aids and the commerce of the people traffickers, the malign progress of slave ships replaced by road trains. The wheels of this industry roll eastward like some massive relief or resupply operation - the Berlin Airlift brought to earth, and a road that sustains so many along its route and through its commerce.

A slide show of uncountable shack bars races past, with occasional repair shops living on the misfortune of travellers. Slow down at all and snack bar cucumber sellers and tea boys suddenly appear for the passing trade. It's the service sector at its most basic. The Morse Code of the car horns constantly signals - a sort of audio Braille, sending messages of greeting, danger, warning, exuberance or threat; their array of greetings, their scale and range ear splitting. On the back of one lorry, the iconic twin pictures of Che Guevara and Bob Marley loom - Politics and Ganga; it's the 60's all over again but with a Jamaican soundtrack.

Some snapshots remain from that trip: by the side of the road the upturned face of concern on the frail wisp of a grandmother, her confusion counselled by a daughter; the rice paddies, oxen ploughed; traffic and goats, lorries and cows; the boy half hanging out the side of the weaving overtaking bus, paid to be a human indicator but scolding another youth for popping his head out, even just a little. Elderly men in Topi hats carry themselves with dignified gait; the woman carrying two bits of wood that looked like replacement chair legs. It's the fetch and carry economy here. Other women appear with great wicker baskets, these herbal backpackers filled to camouflage point. A massive hydro plant on our right followed by women replanting, bent over rice fields.

Stats are rolled out: one woman dies roughly every two hours in childbirth or from related complications. Of course if one wanted to reduce the alarmingly high rates of mother and child mortality in rural areas, it would be helpful if childbirth wasn't seen as an inconvenient and perhaps ritually unclean activity and women weren't sent out to the barn to deliver children with cows and goats as assistant

17

midwives.   Still some distance to travel for the women's movement in Nepal.

After three hours, we're about half way now and we start to meet some glorious lush vegetation and rolling terraces with rice planted fields.   Why is this country not a food exporter?   Perhaps its remoteness and Multinational Agribusiness haven't seen it as a viable concern yet?   However, there is one positive side to this: no McDonalds!

Approaching now is the flat land approaching Pokhara and suddenly it's like driving on corrugated iron, with voices moving into tremolo. The quality of housing also starts to suddenly improve, built by Gurkha comparative wealth.   Our six hour journey finally concludes and we book into the Sacred Valley Guest House by the Lakeside. It's run by Gunga and Ailsa, friends of Philip and Deborah. Ailsa also works as a librarian at KISC. (Kathmandu International Study Centre, a mission school in Kathmandu open to expatriate children from primary to advanced level. KISC has enabled Philip and Deborah to live and work in Kathmandu since 2000. Their two older children have graduated and are now studying in the UK).   We get a discount.   It's a whole 600 rupees a night for a spacious room and en suite. (£6)

I trod in something exiting the car which doesn't want to come off.   Whilst walking later to the restaurant, I mount a step carelessly and knock over a rail of dresses, managing to walk over two of them before embarrassed apologies.   "You still trying to clean your shoes?" Philip helpfully asks.   Perhaps I was thinking of Eddie Izzard's dress codes. As a child, Eddie had briefly lived in the street next to mine and had run 41 marathons in 51 days during the summer of 2009 for Sports Relief. He would fuse with Obama, becoming a mental resource for lots of "Yes I can" positive self talk. Cause if Eddie could.....   When times get really tough, I will also recite the team sheet from NI Espana 82.

18

Great food was consumed later in the Moondance Restaurant: Bruschetta, Tagliatelle and Pizza for us all. The second big bottle of Everest beer was too much for me, I suppose. Relief at having survived the journey, combined with altitude and the stark ageing reality that I can't handle drink any more, all had a sobering effect... the next day! I couldn't seem to turn down the volume on a soundtrack mix of excitement and trepidation at the task ahead. It kept rolling, past lights out. I had a nagging feeling that going up and down Scrabo (a local hill with a monument, located at the head of Strangford Lough, Newtownards, Northern Ireland, a few hundred feet above sea level) a few times perhaps wasn't a demanding enough training programme for what was to unravel tomorrow.

Day 3

Tramp to Dhampus/ Sunlit Uplands/ Sungeeta and Pitchfork

Next morning brings a shopping expedition for a smaller backpack in tourist friendly shop fronts more Greek-like than Indian. In fact, iPokhara's Lakeside is more like any holiday town lacking only in buckets, spades and rounder bats. Necessary provisions are made and we visit to pay for and collect our trekking permits. The Swiss in the queue in front helpfully observes to the clerk, "Can you not read?" when his name is misspelt.

"Clever", I think, "get them on your side!" A rather large Australian woman on my right asks, "Are you excited?" I fake sincerity, say yes, denying the rising anxiety. It's time to hit the trek. Our guide is Purna...so he should know his way round Anna.

A thirty minute taxi ride ends at some nondescript corner facing wooded hills to our right and almost vertical steps that were swallowed too soon by the trees. The awful truth was starting to dawn: 10,000 lung busting steps on the ascent to Dhampus. I do about thirty or so before I need oxygen. This fun continues for the next hour or so, at which point Philip unwisely informs me that there is actually a road to Dhampus. That's the point at which I decide never to quite trust anyone again and to bring out that resentment occasionally and polish it. A man whom I think is in his mid 60s strides past my 15th wheeze stop. Philip informs me he is probably in his mid 40s. It's a hard life here and a short one. I take a mental note: 'walking uphill prematurely ages you'. I discard this note as it's much too late for that lesson to have any practical application. Eventually the verticals peter out and we emerge onto the more gentle slopes of terraced inclines with lush vegetation and tracks onto the village of Dhampus. Bright sunlit uplands would be too Churchillian perhaps, but that's what they were.

We decide on the Anu Guest House, a collection of white brick stone and tin roofs, with 3 double rooms in a block with shower room and toilet rustically at the end. It's really expensive - for a double room it's 400 rupees, nearly £2 each! The rooms are stone floored with simple beds, overlooking a geraniumed rectangular garden section which fell away rapidly to the valley floor 10 miles below and then across to a triple range of ridges forming the opposite slopes. They tempt us with talk of the football on the telly, but the satellite only shows a WWF bout, mercifully cut short by the power cut. The first really cold water arrives, followed by the sweetest tea you've had since your Granny made it. Our guide, Purna passed his wife's previous home on our ascent; now he lives across the valley in the opposite direction to our view, married for 2 years with a 6 month old daughter who cries a lot. My total lack of Nepali and limited range of explanatory gestures quickly run out. The only communicative medium left is music and a shared iPod featuring an Irish selection of U2 and Iona. This seems to go down well as we await a special Dal Bhat, served by the prettiest 10 year old girl in the village, Sungeeta, home from school and straight into the family business. Its 6:30pm and the light is going fast as we hungrily await the meal, at least partially prepared by what we think is the family's youngest daughter, Sungeeta.

Sungeeta, it emerges, has found a home in the Anu Hotel; she's from a nearby village. Her mother ran away to another part of the country last year with a new partner and her father retaliated and did the same, but without the bus journey. Sungeeta then became persona non grata. She was taken in by the owners of the Anu, who send her to school. "She's part of our family now", the man explains. He pays for her schooling and she works in the hotel - a benign example of child labour. The Dal Bhat arrives - the usual meal of rice, with lentils (Dal) and a range of curried vegetables. This local staple diet is served up twice a day, bookending light and twilight. Mega extra portions arrive and are ladled. Nouvelle cuisine hasn't caught on here for a dish that is designed to fill, rather than providing any great range of taste.

Repairing to bed at about 11 and it's all quiet apart from western breathing. I am awoken by a distant 4 note ram's horn, no doubt played by some demented town crier rival of the cockerel, greeting the passing of the night! It continues and moves relentlessly closer. I check my watch; it's only 1:30! I can hear a rap chant now accompanying the horn section. This routine is repeated again and again until he's outside our door, ram chanting and shining his torch rapidly from left to right, no doubt wishing us all the best. This has caught Philip completely by surprise - a nice little wake up call. I resist the temptation to rise and remark, "I say, this is a terribly inconvenient time to call. Could we diarise another opportunity for you to visit...perhaps after I fly home?" Instead I lie still, breath holding for the minute it takes him to perform and move on through the village to his next gig. Hindu holy men apparently are light sleepers and thus prone to such nocturnal activities, encouraging villagers to rise and offer alms. It gets him off your doorstep, you don't get cursed and you get a blessing instead. It doesn't help in forming long term relationships though.

Earlier in the day, a robed holy man clutching a little non nuclear Trident had accosted us at breakfast, requesting alms. He is offered

21

food but that apparently is a break of protocol; he can only take travellers cheques, Visa, Maestro or equivalent to buy said food. No financial donations were offered. We see him an hour later in another part of town. Perhaps Pitchfork is tracking us, bringing good cheer. It's not immediately easy to return to sleep.

I plot revenge for next time. I hear the approaching rant/chant and creep out into the bushes. At the opportune moment, I unleash my smuggled Tazer on his butt and ruthlessly increase the voltage until he whistles Dixie. I deny the possibility of his comeback curse which causes testicular shrivelling and some nasty ticks. Maybe I'll just let it go!

Day 4

The Attack of the Rat Plaster/ Ulster Methane/Rum Cracker/ Knees up/ Landruk/ Facilities/ the Attack/ Language Lesson

> Q to game show contestant: "What's the force of nature that keeps one from drifting off the earth and up into the atmosphere?"
>
> Ans: "Delta Force."

Over breakfast of omelette and sweet Gurung bread, Philip recounts a previous group encounter with a holy man. The pilgrim shows his trident and alms tin to a group at breakfast. A rather confrontational mostly bald Northerner with pony tail responds by producing his cross on neckless, shaking it at Trident and stating repeatedly, "I'm a Krristiann." It's strident versus Trident. The confused holy man then has a moment of enlightenment, taking off all his accoutrements and opening his robe to reveal a great variety of intricate symbolic weavings round his genitalia. An unfortunate case of 'you've shown me yours, so now I'll show you mine!' Luckily most of breakfast had been consumed!

The day had dawned with Fish Tail just about visible, before the heat haze rose over the valley and obscured the views. At 7am, three young boys were already hollowing out another terrace, 200 metres away. I note that last night's Dal Bhat was a very efficient methane producer, with enough to power up a small to medium sized enterprise. Thank goodness there were no naked lights. Another Ulsterman applied this thought in the 1960's but made a more useful connection by developing the design of the Anaerobic Digester whereby animal dung is fed into an underground tank and allowed to settle and ferment, producing methane, which is then siphoned off as fuel to power lights and heat. It' now used in villages throughout Asia!

On receipt of the bill, one strange item is queried - Rum Cracker! Go on, fess up, who's been at the secret VAT of rum? This prompts all sorts of Frank Carson impersonations a la 'It's a cracker" etc. Sadly it turns out only to be 'Room Charges' but we still look for grade A rum surprise at the next lodge!

> Handy Himalayan Hint: Never rush past a toilet without due care and reflection and never trust flatulence!

On past some more lush vegetation, with up hills and down dals on a stepped descent that goes on for more than an hour. The uneven steps mean one can't relax into a rhythm and I find that descending like this puts a whack of pressure on the old knees. At the valley floor we stop for some ritual insults, with the kind hostess wondering how people so fat could even walk. Of course their advice is that nevertheless, we should remain there for refuelling, as it's three days

23

until the next pit stop and we'll still need to eat, in order to have any chance of getting there before emaciation. We decline this warm hearted concern, buy a bottle of water and pant onwards. Neither Philip nor I are insubstantial in girth, though I'm convinced I'm anorexic, cause every time I look in the mirror I see a fat man staring back at me. Time to ascend. Of course for every ascent there's invariably an equal and opposite descent. It's a law of nature, if not a force ...like Delta Force!

We are taking too many breaks and I learn a new Nepali word, "Jum" which means "Get up off your ass and get it into gear". Remarkably fulsome advisory content for a three letter word! A bit more up and then lots of down, past another village at which point I cleverly decide to jump from a 3ft wall and immediately realise a major mistake as right knee shouts out in pain. This could slow the next sheer descent. We decide to send Purna on ahead to book us into a suitable hostelry in Landruk as whole clutches of trekkers are out and about today, plus the weather looks a bit threatening.

Another hour and we arrive at the village of Landruk, collapsing onto the beds of the Super View Guest House. "Brad Pitt wasn't here" is scrawled on the toilet wall. The hotel is filling up quickly as the rain descends. (We find out next morning that they had cleverly moved the direction of the village signpost, hence the 'No Vacancies...No Irish' notice soon appears!)

I am apprised on the facilities through the question, "Which is worse...a shower that only runs cold..a broken toilet seat...or a toilet that doesn't flush?" It's a Hmm ilayan par three and I eventually plump for the third horror. You're allowed one objection, but voice two and you're sent home in disgrace. The toilet window frame without a window didn't even make it onto the list. It seems in our eagerness to flop on a bed we did not study the small print sufficiently and our en suite facilities were those of the economy room. Another 100 rupees would have brought the delights of a hot shower and perhaps glass in the window. No guarantee of flushing toilet though!

Philip flops down after his refreshing shower to be bombarded by falling stringy things caused by heavy booted foreigner upstairs. He thinks immediately it was a rat attack but it's just the attack of the rat plaster.

I begin to think we are acting out a Father Ted Lenten script where breakfast was a bowl of cold water; he is forced to sleep on a brick mattress and is thrashed with branches. I see you Father and I raise you with……..

Time to order evening meal. The cookhouse here is constructed out of corrugated iron, venting steam and smoke from the roofing joint like some down at heel roadhouse. While waiting, it's time for a Nepali language lesson:

> Dania Bhad, pronounced Dhanybad: Thank you
>
> China: No (Ulster says China?)
>
> Ho (not Yo!): Yes
>
> Chia: Tea
>
> "Deri Ramro" - Very Good (don't annoy Derry Rambo cause you'll make him angry hey)

Eggy delights and Momos are ordered. They take an hour rather than a minute. No fast food here as fresh is best! We chat with a German lady who lives in Greece and bemoans the living beyond their means. She wrecked her knee in a car accident a couple of years ago and this is her first big test drive. She very much wants to make it to ABC (Annapurna Base Camp) but if the knee doesn't hold out then at least she has tried. My money is on the "she made it" end of the equation. I decide not to mention my own rather pathetic limping.

We're exhausted post food at 7:00pm, after the six hours on the trail. Sadly in bed by 7:15pm but happily sleep on and off until 6am. The last time that happened, I think I was twelve. We vow never to disclose how early the early night was. I used to be allowed to stay up until 7:30pm to see Z Cars or Top of the Pops. Now my life is in reverse and the spectre of daughter visiting to shoo me off to bed with a promise to call up and read me a story later, looms alarmingly.

Day 5

Don't mention Basil Fawlty/ Showers/ Landslides/ Knees up to Ghandruk/ Lato/Shangri La/ Mountains/ Young German/John Cleese/ Hot Foot/ Billy/ AM

An early morning cold shower gets one's attention. Highly recommended ...for your enemies. The ritual clearing of throats occurs apace, helping to keep TB right up there as a major infectious disease in Nepal. Timely diversion occurs via a breakfast of the most gorgeous porridge with fruit, which should provide sufficient retro power to assist with the ascent. It's time to face a traverse down to the very bottom of the valley floor, across a Gurkha bridge and straight up to Ghandruk at 1950 metres above sea level. This is the one that filled me with fear of failure, so in search of a courage top up, I pulled on my replica 1982 NI World Cup shirt, hoping for inspiration from the memory of Billy's Boys. They say it'll take 4.5 hours.

The massive landslide opposite prompts a conversation on a proposal from some of Philip's colleagues to get dog tags. "Did you notice the earthquake box at the house and the whistle? You could shout for a few hours but you can whistle for days", he quips. Of course there is a fine line between comfortable preparedness and paranoia but Nepal is right on an earthquake fault line. Haiti has shocked many and one colleague has packed her bags and plans to leave.

The walk down through Landruk takes us past the rather angular Peaceful Restaurant, which is anchored with guy ropes and perched on the edge of a sheer drop. I can't imagine it offering one an evening without anxiety. A Trident reaches upwards from where a weather vane should be. Hmm...another calling card?

A woman hurries past us making a delivery, holding to her right hip a large metal bowl of cooked rice and on her upturned left hand, a seemingly plaited little mountain shape of dung. It really would have been the yang of a dream topping! Maybe it was a present, but as Philip observed, "I'm sure she'll wash her hands thoroughly afterwards!" The left hand really is used for ablutive functions here. Some experts claim that the regular simple use of carbolic soap could reduce instances of dietary diseases and bowel infections by up to 50%.

An old man ascends wearing green canvas shoes which are very common here. Unsurprisingly then, the Maoists in their campaign used green canvas shoes as part of their uniform. Many leprosy sufferers also wore this footwear and were often delayed at army checkpoints on their way to hospital appointments at the INF (International Nepal Fellowship) clinic in Jumla. "The army think we're Maoists", they reported. Consequently, INF got blue canvas shoes for leprosy outpatients and informed the authorities. They seemed to then get through in double quick time!

One third of the way on the ascent to Ghandruk, two middle aged Japanese men are descending. We exchange good mornings. "You going up to Ghandruk?" they ask. It was sort of obvious ...but we confirm. They start to laugh but without the bonhomie of shared fun and games. Philip refuses to let that one go and is compelled to remind them, "Now you go down...but then you go UP"! We all laugh again, but this time with more equanimity. Remember Tenko!

On my way up this most sheer sustained ascent so far, I comfort myself with the thought that apparently smokers (I'm an ex) perform better at 3000m and above. That's why I'm so rubbish at sea level, I need the vertical limit. I'm off them 13 years, 4 months and 3 days but I don't miss them. I stop to pant and purchase water and a man in his 30's or 40's comes down the steps on his hands, legs horribly twisted underneath him. It's like a western where civil war amputees hand shuffle along the boardwalks. But here it's the person who's called "Useless" or "Lato", not his legs. He could well have fallen out of a tree when he was younger. There are no NHS clinics nearby.

Philip then recounts a tale from 8 years ago where a man who had fallen out of a tree as a child had similarly broken his legs and not been able to access a hospital. He was put into a corner and by the time he was brought to Grace Church in Kathmandu, he was at such a low point he didn't even speak. Others spoke for him. He also had lost his 'usefulness'. The Pastor that Saturday preached a sermon on Peter and John entering the Temple and their response to the crippled beggar, when asked for money.... 'Silver and Gold have I none but what I have I give to thee'. A group were asked to pray over him. After about 45 minutes of this, Philip was amongst this group who then lifted him up and his legs seemed to experience some sort of release or muscular spasm as they descended. He couldn't walk but over the next 2 months, he was taken to rehabilitation, progressed into a wheelchair and eventually was able to walk back to his village in the hills. He just needed some care and prayer. A Down's Syndrome teen was also there at this stop point. They suffer the same judgement of "useless" but thankfully this boy's mother was a strong character and he attended the local school. Definitely not one who was hidden away.

We are almost there now and see a sign that says "Eco Guest House".

The heavens open 5 minutes from our Guest House and we take shelter in a Didi's (older sister's) porch. She kindly ushers us to seats and we wait it out for 10 minutes. A drier dander resumes and a boy suddenly thrusts a rolled up cigarette of small notes at me, no explanation offered. I resist the temptation to reach and take it with a thank you. Others had asked earlier for sweets in rising and angry crescendo. One begins to beware of the 'Namaste' greeting offered by children, as it's usually a tutored precursor to "Sweets" or "Money" or ""Very hungry".

Namaste, pronounced Namus Day: 'We greet the God within you'.

Ghandruk is a traditional Gurung village of Long Houses, two storied elongated collective structures facing at right angles to each other, with white and black beams painted, reminiscent of a certain stretched Elizabethan ambience. Running a video of Property Market Abroad, I see upstairs living quarters with a cosy, amenable and rustic charm, in a prime location close to all major mountain ranges amenities with downstairs storage for animals and supplies. Some Ambi Pur plug-ins will deal with any unwelcome odours! A value alternative to the Dordogne, my brochure says, with lots of wheat, potatoes and vegetables appearing on any available plot of ground.

We've finally arrived at the Shangri La Guest House, run by another Gunga (you couldn't make it up!) and shirts dripping with sweat and rain, we ascend to the upper veranda. I should really have then inducted Purna into first high altitude NI Affiliated Supporters Club. Hand on badge, he could have recited the sacred pantheon of: Jimmy McIlroy, Danny Blanchflower, Billy Bingham, Norman Uprichard (bias there) the Doog, Geordie Best, Gerry Armstrong, Billy Hamilton, Big Pat, Sammy McIlroy, Martin O'Neill and David Healy, finally to pledge that we will remember them and seal it with a cup of steaming black tea.

Everyone remembers where they were when a vital goal was scored, and perhaps maybe when Kennedy was shot or Diana crashed. Gerry Armstrong against Spain in Valencia and David Healy against England in 2005 are obvious candidates but I have another one: Madrid 1st July 1982, in the Vincente Calderon stadium. We're 2-1 down against Austria in the quarter finals of the World Cup with 15 minutes to go in 100 degrees of heat. We keep pressing, with hearts of lions, unwilling to admit the dream might be coming to an end. The ball is poked forward on the right and Jimmy Nicholl pounds after it on the overlap, right to the edge of the box. Their keeper, Koncilia, has a rush of blood and races out. Jimmy gets there first and loops it over into the left hand corner of the six yard box. It hangs in the air in frame by frame ultra slow motion (in fact in a parallel universe it's still hanging there), finally arriving and met on the head of Billy Hamilton, who had moved forward in hope and expectation. At 45 degrees he connects, the ball headed downwards, just in front of the line and taking 2 hours to go through the legs of a floundering Austrian defender.

Right behind the goal a group of Norn Iron fans erupt with joy. John, a Crusaders fan, runs round in demented celebratory decreasing circles waving his NI pennant. A group leap up and down again and again, with hands raised in surrender to the moment. Glasses fly off and we all swell with pride. A kind bemused Spaniard hands my glasses back. That's the one I treasure, with a freeze frame shutter recall from 20 feet behind the goal. Billy Hamilton, scorer of a brace that day, gave so much and was so dehydrated that water had to be sponged into his skin on the physio table. Remembering such giants of men, I flop onto the lodge bed, rather too like that Father Ted penitential brick bed, but I didn't feel a thing! My mind on things that matter; made it!

Heaven has crisp white sheets, Spartan but clean rooms, with welcoming black tea and a backdrop of suddenly materialising Machhapuchhare and the Annapurnas. The thunder, lightning and downpour have cleared the mists from the heights and for the first time, the majestic views appear. Philip is ecstatic at their appearance and the cameras start to whirl. Apparently some people have lived for years in Nepal and have never seen this. The sun breaks through and evokes a desire to reach out, just like Diana Ross and touch somebody's hand. As there are no women around, I hold that one in check. Instead I reach out to the mountains.

There is a promise of a hot shower so I seek to avail of this luxury while the electricity's on. Expectantly, I turn the red; it's cool, remains cool and becomes almost lukewarm after a few minutes. Needing it badly, I dab and scrub, getting a layer of gunge off and, shivering, report false information, "No hot here!" Philip tries and 20 minutes later comes back, reddened and hot flushed by the experience and also terribly smug. "Did you try the blue tap... because the colour coding means nothing here?" Now he tells me! "Blue can be hot or cold, and the red also, it depends." There's obviously a need for an Asian plumbing charter mark for the showers in the lodges of Nepal. I can't face the disappointment if I go back and find......

A group of German Trekkers arrive but for once my towel is out before theirs. After a satisfying collapse and stretch on the edge of sleep for 20 minutes, I arise feeling a bit more chipper. Replete with beer, beard and issues, a young German (henceforth YG) with feet up on the veranda rail hails me, and asks, "How are you?"

"I'm good!", I genuinely reply.

"Just good?" he follows up.

"No, really good ..brilliantly good", I elucidate. I can feel this is going somewhere interesting.

"Are you English?" YG asks.

Not wanting to stir Volk memories of our back to back wins against them in 1983 or get into political nuance, I say "No...Irish". I ask where he is from and he tells me he is German. I ask how he is.

He tells me, "Vere exhausted after a gruelling 14 day trek. But Ve Germans like ze pain."

Organised pain, I think but don't say; though I do say, "You can get help for that you know." He carries on about their dedication to pain and discomfort. "No, you really can get help for that you know."

He looks at me quizzically and asks, "Vere? In Ireland?"

I say, "Yes...after a couple of pints of Guinness, you'll never want to work again."

He then asks if we've also been trekking? I say, "Yes and I'm really, really exhausted too and sore all over."

"How long for?"

"Three days," I say. He is unsure how to respond and I quickly pop back into our room where McMillan is stuffing a towel in his mouth to control his tittering over a potential international incident.

Later on YG's mother appears shivering in the dining room

downstairs. "I need heat", she says. I talk about our so cold long winter, the worst since our big snow of 1963 and how it was 8 degrees when I left. "Below?" she asks. " It was -2 in Munich two weeks ago." I change the subject quickly to occupations. She worked in admin. I mention I was a teacher and had escaped for the Easter break via a tunnel...burrowing out under the wire. Thankfully I didn't mention searchlights and watchtowers. With flushing discomfort, I again realise the spirit of Basil Fawlty is hovering at my shoulder, coaxing out inappropriate analogies. Get thee behind me Basil! (July note: Of course in a sort of muted retaliation, some Germans have been heard to say, "Don't mention the 4", after Germany's clinical despatch of England in South Africa!)

More Germans arrive. Thankfully there was football. Engaging with a very personable Borussia Monchengladbach fan, I ask about ticket prices in the Bundesliga. He tells me they are between 15 and 17 Euros! Average attendance at Borrusia Dortmund was over 76,000 in 2009. I tell him that to see Chelsea, the cheap seats start at £80. For Manchester United it's a snip at £52. He is staggered by that, as I am by the value he enjoys. It truly is a people's game there and confirms something very rotten in the state of English football.

Gunga has joined us across the table. We have eaten mightily of pasta and cheese dishes with just a hint of spice and edge. Philip struggles to finish his vegetarian spaghetti alla Bolognese. This is indeed a feat for our hosts. Gunga limps heavily on his bandaged right foot which he says he has broken today. It may well indeed be broken as Philip recounted a case earlier of a Sherpa presenting himself to a local doctor complaining of a sore neck. It turned out to be broken. These Gurung people provide one of the main recruiting sources for the Gurkhas, along with their rivals, the Magars. They are an incredibly strong people, ascending the steps, regularly carrying loads of 25-35 kg. I don't know if anyone's been mugged by a Gurkha but I advise against resistance as that would be futile.

His misfortune is indeed our opportunity...to get warm. We all sit round a table that will comfortably seat 20 with what looks like a thick blanket adorning the sides and reaching down to the floor with foot rests underneath. Then Gunga's wife comes in with a bucket of hot ashes and throws it into what we see is a large pit running the length and breadth underneath the dining table. That's the central heating kicking in on a cold evening. We are encouraged to lift the sides, place it on our knees and discover a wonderful warming glow toasting feet and picking up the mood. The mood of the Sherpas at the other end of the table had already risen, in proportion to their consumption of the local poteen, Rakshi. Now they were warm on the outside as well. I've only encountered one foreign poteen and that was at a match at Windsor Park. It was Albanian and called Rickya. And that's what it did - Wreck Ya! Temporary blindness ensued and when that cleared, I thought we were Brazil, not Northern Ireland. Ricya, Rakshi, Raki (in Georgia) all must be under some sort of international licence available in local variable franchise. Very clever, this identifiable cross cultural branding got right. Apparently in the depth of winter, guests often stay the night down here and sleep by the heat in a sort of Himalayan lock in. It's time to retire from the table before we slump into our tea. Or perhaps given the circumstances, beat a retreat.

> Handy Hint: Don't wear cheap thin trainers when getting your feet under the table. When they melt, the smell is awful!

Suddenly a drumming band starts up, rivalling any Orange Lambeg. The clashing cymbals add to the decibels. Perhaps it's a celebration of a wedding or a local deity or they've heard there's a couple of Ulster prods (or in true Little Britain style, the only Ulster prods) in the village, and they're conducting a welcoming homage. Nepalis do so much want to make you feel at home. Their routine doesn't vary much though. It's one two, one two, one… one…the default keep time rhythm when the flutes were at rest. I wave at them from the veranda but the portal to July 1964 remains decidedly closed and I'm not sent forth with a bag of oranges for my uncle Billy. They were the only fruit then. It would have been helpful if my Aunt had not just shouted out ,"Billy" and seventy per cent of the Lodge turned round.

Eight years later and that day's experience was re applied. It was March 1972 and the Stormont government had just been abolished the previous evening with Direct Rule imposed from London. The whole shipyard workforce walked out and paraded through Belfast in protest, passing my office block. In a classic case of mistiming, two catholic colleagues and I were just out on our lunch break. We were the only ones in High Street moving in the opposite direction to the protest parade, perhaps evidencing a divergent religious or political persuasion (same thing here) and began attracting some rather nasty and dangerous looks. Being proactive, I found myself raising a right hand, as it was now my turn to shout "Billy!" This time, many eyes turned quizzically and suspiciously in our direction but thankfully a couple of men waved back and we turned quickly down a side street and escaped.

Back to 2010 and a night of broken sleep follows on a mattress that must have been at least half an inch thick. A 2am trip to the loo sees a braw bright night with star clusters and the moon, the only illumination in a cloudless sky, giving a surreal view of blue rinsed white mountains luminous in the night air, a giant backdrop canvas in 3D, towering and revealing all their glory. Machhapuchhare is a holy mountain and no one is allowed to climb it. Some Bedechi (foreigner) tried to in 1963 and fell to his death. Perhaps there's a giant angel guardian up there, who swept him off with a luminous sword, saying there's some places you don't go and which you can't conquer, like this giant negative print of shining austere sentinels in the perfect still.

Earlier, I had asked Philip, "What does it mean to you, seeing these mountains out?"

"I never grow bored with them", he answered, and "I never cease to marvel. I think of Psalm 121: 'I lift up my eyes to the hills, from where does my help come'...and that writer saw nothing as majestic as these. And the little plants beside the paths here...they also are

35

majestic. The same God made them both." Majesty and detail, and in the detail.

The cold ends the musing but the gaze is long enough to burn it on the retina plate behind the eyes, a permanent imprint, available for recall even now. Ghandruk is 1950m above sea level and is above the winter snow line, therefore I've walked above the snow line in the Himalayas…but not when it was snowing. Does that count?

> <u>Handy Hint:</u> Try to ensure your sleeping bags are hermetically sealed.

Day 6: (1)

Sun up and down dale/ Mountain Morning/ Aussies/ Retreat/ Royal Ulster Fry/ Lengthening the Stride/ Nayapul/ Taxi?

In the morning I'm up well before 6:00 and race to the shower in order to get the hot first, before gazing at mountain sunrise. I turn the blue on.....cold! I turn the red on; it's cold! I punch in the code and repeat the combinations..angrily! No combination works and I enjoy another bracing shower. Perhaps it was all used last night by Philip and the Germans! Hot water's elusive in Gurkha land. I entertain a lurking suspicion though that there may be a little man downstairs in the boiler room. He keeps switching a lever, moving the points and reversing the polarity of the plumbing, just to confuse the tourist. I go down and check… but there's no one there.

Dawn spreads between 5:30 and 6:00. Purna is also up with tea and we chastened trekkers gaze at the reveal in a dazed wonder. Their true glory that is always there, even when mist shrouded, is now beginning to appear.

By 6:10 the first glimpses of sun hit the upper edges, reddening the rim and setting off vapour in steamy wisps of factory smoke. This repeats along the peaks. The haze then gathers round Fishtail as its outlines are softened by the vapour. The dark green of the hills starkly contrasts with the pure white of the peaks and on the left, a triangular ridge like the back of an enormous armoured lizard provides a bridge, taking the eye from lush green to white. The village is up and about. Dogs bark and food preparation H style is underway. A late cockerel sends a greeting signal whilst Annapurna 2 gives off more wreaths of smoke. The ritual clearing of throats occurs and the mundane normalities of life restart, even in the shadow of such power and wonder. A portion of rice has been harvested from the patch in front of us, as here all is for use; no ground is wasted in this recycling culture, the envy of Greens everywhere. The struggle and work of it all is less envious though.

The cycle of revelation continues further. It's in front of such as these mountains that mouths stop, words fail, jaws drop and all the detritus of anxiety over money, status and possessions falls away. Success, failure, regrets, angers, clashes and the world, as only through my eyes fall away, to reveal a world of stark beauty that has existed long before and will remain long after our anxious passage through it. It's against this beauty that it's all measured.

6:35: The ascent of the Sun begins and we start a fresh page... seeking to expand the lungs, to breathe in more and widen the eyes to somehow see more clearly. We're handed a bill of 1600 rupees for room and evening feast. It must have been the tally chart of teas that drove up the price.

We set off early, at 6:50 with only tea taken, wanting to avoid, at least for a while, the shame of being overtaken on the long slow descent to Nayapul (New Bridge) by our fitter German friends. Just a little way down this narrow track, we hug the inside lane as a mule re supply train ascends, replete with jangling bells that, in addition to acting as a horn, keeping the attention of the pack and making sure their handlers know where they are, apparently ward off evil spirits, especially in forests at night. If you've no bell you just ...give a little whistle.

We crack on for a couple of hours, hearing no Teutonic tones echoing behind. I do hear a hackle in preparation behind me at one stage and hasten my step even more. We meet a large group of Aussies just a few hours into their 14 day trek. They offer us little sympathy as I ham up our four day ordeal, branding us "Typical Poms." There's mock outrage from us...then we're identified as Scots...and finally Irish. It made them happy, so I didn't go into the complexities of Northern Irish overlapping identities. Of course then everyone's Granny was Irish and their sons were all called Declan so we offer discounts on accommodation. I discover we are in effect 'Poms by association', which in a way neatly describes our complex political status. A little further on, a group of Japanese reminds us, after hellos, that they are ermm...Japanese, just in case we thought they were perhaps... Dutch. We wish hopeful real Dutch trekkers good fortune in the World Cup...this is their year, they say. Great if it was; the greatest team never to win it.

After this Internationale, we finally draw breath and reach a restaurant stop at 9:30. At 10:00, YG comes striding into view, deposits backpack outside and flexes arms and shoulders in warm down. My heart sinks; they've caught up. At the other end of the veranda, we slide a little lower in our chairs and lose our cheer a little as the hound closes on the fox. After a few minutes, no others appear and I regain some hope. Then another of their party arrives. We quickly shuffle into gear and move on just as they enter the veranda...wishing them a good breakfast. We are then told infuriatingly by YG that, " No...Ve just drink tea!" Hmm...masterful hardy souls. In this downhill trekking contest between Royal Ulster Fry and super fit super race, our strategic withdrawal moves on with renewed vigour. As one General has perceptively pointed out, the hardest operation any army can carry out is a fighting retreat, holding their shape, whilst in contact with a ruthless enemy. I check my roll of fat and confirm yep...still holding my shape... and resume the retreat.

Further down the track, we pound for two solid hours and more, lengthening our stride, purposeful and renewed, we are now almost at riverside and the ground becomes even. Our porter suddenly develops a sore leg and wants to slow. In such dire straits as these, we may have to consider leaving our wounded behind, but he recovers. A slow decline to Nayapul continues with the sound of rushing water in my left ear for two hours as we track the river bed. As we descend, so many more come up from Nayapul. All ascending commerce is via the fetch and carry economy of the back or placement on mules. A boy no more than 4 feet high has a folded 8feet sheet of corrugated iron strapped to his back. A man carries a sack of rice, another one with impossibly large rolls of electrical conduit. We're almost out and we pass a teenage girl, sitting automaton like on a cart full of small rocks, contemplating a career of pounding and breaking them into gravel size.

We emerge into the frontier town of Nayapul, a harsh hard re acquaintance with a form of civilisation demanding of care and suspicion. On a bit further, to the slow incline with small car taxis lined up. They operate in a 'who's waited the longest' queue. A 20 year old states the price of 1500 rupees; he's next. He drives a brown Corolla a lot older than himself. Philip feels it may not have a completely up to date MOT and allied with the surly nature of the youth and the lack of road quality, he wants an older man and a more modern car. An animated debate begins as we attempt to break their protocol. The snarling youth prevents other drivers taking us and his stand off only ends when a man in his 40's appears, taking over and allocating the next in line. Seniority rules and we climb into a rather rustic little Suzuki with plastic flower garland draped round the inside and picture of a special pagoda on the dash but no choice of rice or chips.

Later that night in Pokhara, I meet the Borussia Monchengladbach fan. They had set off at 7:45. "You left so early", he observed with a hint of shock. They arrived at Nayapul at 12:30...half an hour after us. We were plucked from the riverside just in the nick of time by a fleet of little taxis spread out in a line, stretching into distance. A little bit of honour retained.

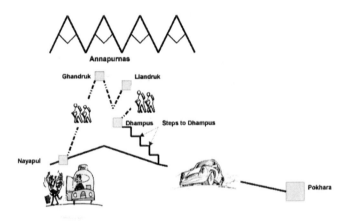

The Route....

Day 6 (2)
Bag Ladies/ Tiffin/ Between the Worlds/ Van the Man

About 1:30, we arrive back at the Sacred Valley, after another hair rising taxi ride of an hour or so, negotiating the tarmac between the potholes. This driver was quite good; he only tried to write us off once in between the ongoing games of chicken. I think he thinks it's expected! At the conclusion, Purna offers us head towel gifts as a present. I get a green Bob Marley, so I suppose every little thing's gonna be all right. Despite his smile though, his rather sad eyes seem to belie that.

We stumble forward from the tiny taxi and on into the cool surroundings of the Sacred Valley, run by Gunga Wynn. I think he must be from Pontypridd. I head for the shower and turn the blue tap. It starts and then remains cold. Perhaps there is no hot, or perhaps they've switched the points again to confuse Jonnie foreigner. 'Try red', a voice inside cries whereupon steam and bliss obliterate the heat and the dust. Shower Wars...episode 6: The return of the Red Aye.

A banana muffin that has descended from the bakery on Mount Olympus allies with filter coffee that invokes recent memory. After 4 days of black mountain tea, it intoxicatingly swirls round the taste buds. Time is short though, so at 3:00 we taxi off to the Women's Bag Factory, a Nepali Fair Trade organisation for community groups. My heart sinks just a little at the prospect of forced purchase of a man bag. Stiff upper lip though. However, when getting there, we find an oasis of industry, purpose and dignity fuelled by a mix of private and public funding. Who said that couldn't work? Leave it all to the invisible hand of the markets without morals, or the regulated joyless stride of the collective? Instead we have dynamism, energy and innovation. Many of their goods have already appeared back in NI via FONIC house parties. There are 400 core members of the Co-op, with 80 at any one time actually on the premises, the rest being outworkers who weave to order in their villages. A member has to wait 2/3 years to get voting rights, this time lag erecting a

41

necessary barrier against attempted takeovers by one faction or another.

A roaring wood kiln is heating the dye, and a few metres away, hand hanging and laying, then spinning and stitching creative output;, all result in bursting storage rooms. The founder, Mrs Ramkhali Kadka, pride without prejudice, talks of all faiths: Hindu, Muslim and now even some Christians as part of the Co-op. They don't have Christmas Day off here, but in a portent of things to come, a tinselled circular decoration with trailing stars hangs over the door of the factory shop. Perhaps that will make people feel better about working on the 25th, as will the Christmas tree they set out in the centre garden.

I am drawn to the Rates and Regulations sign and the provision of breaks, food and benefits. The ghost of Kenneth Williams tells me that Tiffin (a lunchtime break snack) will be provided. An Australian lady with husband and two Sari'd children in tow hurries breathlessly, lemon tea in hand, from one briefing to another. She can't talk ...she runs a Fair Trade shop in Melbourne, all lean and intense, impeccably eco dressed and driven to drink further from this well. I flounder in the wake of her excitement. Our visit ends with our own lemon tea and brochure to take back to John of Clanrye Trading, who orders up stock from a number of producers. With humility, I ask if I can take a picture of the human dynamo that is Mrs Khali Kadka? Bursting with pride in achievements and without a hint of vanity, she graciously accepts and we bid our farewells. A dinner is planned for the next night with a Pentecostal couple. I request that there be no jiggery Pokhara!

We decide to walk back to the hotel, because I really need the exercise and turn into a long meandering street, past a modern kitchen corner store, next to a welding shop, beside the scrap metal yard and then a sweet kiosk; the usual. The late afternoon haze descends and across the road at the butchers, they sweep up the evidence of a fresh kill. Chickens are mounted in a row on a table top as here most people don't have fridges, making shopping a daily necessity. Meeting the basic needs of subsistence is so very time-consuming; at the standpipe, the waiting line of people with plastic containers immediately gives confirmation.

What is needed is a massive government programme of infrastructure investment, furnishing power grids for all and the means of even basic refrigeration and automated washing; an infrastructure that will aid commercial development. But that's exactly what's not in place - an effective state sector that can enable the private small scale diffused entrepreneurial system that demonstrably can move people and then whole communities forward. Of course there is power to some, but only for 12 hours out of each 24. That's another story! (See Friday)!

I stop to tie my laces, am separated from my companions and human traffickers descend seeking body parts. But after the briefest of inspections, they throw me back. A cow wanders down the centre aisle of the road; the traffic continues to flow round it. Another cow flops down on the grass verge, folds its front legs right over left in a rather camp gesture, takes out a cigarette, and lights up as if to say, "I've done enough today. I'm doing no more!"

We reach the lake and will skirt it to get back to Sacred Valley. Rrrighto boyo? A gleaming slate and granite slab walkway appears lakeside. It was commenced a couple of years ago by the Young Communist League (Maoist) to provide employment via a public works programme. They then ran out of funds and the YCL 'visited' local shop holders with suggestions they make a contribution towards further work. They thought this was a very reasonable request and responded appropriately. 500m later, the path ends abruptly with ridged dried lakeside mud providing an ankle snapping alternative for the rest of the journey. For a moment we were beside Lakes Garda or Ontario, then through a mystic doorway back to the caked earth of lakeside. You step between the worlds with a stride in Pokhara.

43

On to Café Concerto again. Life's so tough here, with a taste packed Bolognese and short walk to Moondance just for desserts. It's similar to the Sacred Valley story; a mix of hippy trail 1970's lady married to a local and then a combined entrepreneurial drive. Mention in Lonely Planet ensures Moondance is brimmed to capacity even on a Wednesday night. But with Egyptian trance jazz in the sound system, it's all too moderne for me. However, it's a welcome change from the mournful dirges in Concerto. "Van the Man inspires Restaurateurs in Pokhara", cries the imaginary headline. Not bad for an East Belfast boy; we travel well.

Day 7:

Exiles/ Airwaves/ Carpenter's Footsteps in the Bus Park

It's April Fools' Day and in another bout of fooling around, the lights go out at 6am. Heading up to the roof terrace of Sacred Valley, the three flights of stairs set off a bout of PTSD but it can all be fixed with the proper cuppa. Obama's Health Care initiative is causing concern for an American lady. She is amazed we might believe in free health care at the point of need. I wonder if this is another April fool but realise she's serious. We reserve the right to cling to our wet Liberal belief in the principles of the NHS and the mixed economy...a slightly different mix to the Sarah Palin recipe though.

Deborah meanwhile had been working on her very own Health Initiative while we had been away. She will look at the issues of healthcare in a Christian Biblical context for use with older/younger women's Bible study groups, which are the norm in Nepali churches. For example, an early session looks at Psalm 139 re truths about how God made our bodies and it shows he cares for us in detail. The session then goes into ante- natal care - immunisation and

44

cleanliness, and also then looks at 1 Timothy 4 v 7,8 have nothing to do with godless myths and old wives' tales, looking for the danger signs in pregnancy. Each session is in two parts, Biblical principle and health advice (with an application of UNICEF guidelines). She's writing 10 sessions, looking at the spiritual and the practical, combating or undermining many of the very unhealthy local practices and traditions, especially round childbirth.

It's a big commitment in time - one more commitment to squeeze into, what seem to me, days already packed full.

Post 'Tea Party', I ask my hosts what makes an entrepreneur. Is it a gifting? Probably...yes, but you can also work at it and develop it. Philip maintains a risk taker can calculate the odds of profit in his head. It's got nothing to do with formal education. We briefly muse on the notion of how to deal with poverty and debt and then wonder how the ancient Israeli aspirational social system portrayed through the Year of Jubilee might have applicability to moderne social and business scenarios: Discuss. However, more pressingly we have a morning/day full of projects to visit. Keith Smith at the Tibetan Refugee Camp, Paulas Panday at YWAM and Chunman Harijan who works with street kids.

We head off through the hidden, less glamorous, non tourist part of town, a bit like the hidden trashy other Niagara Falls. The bus to Bagar departs and we pass the sign to the Bat Cave. Mr Wayne's secret is no more! I met a few real life undercover superheroes that day though.

11am: Keith and Tenzin

Keith Smith helps run Wonder Products of which the Rasillo juice factory is one. Unassuming in baseball cap, jeans and ear ring, he begins our tour. He's set up in the centre of a Tibetan refugee camp of about 1000 people, established on the outskirts of Pokhara. In 1950, the Chinese invaded and then annexed Tibet. The Dalai Llama eventually fled in 1959 to Dharamsala, north of New Delhi to lead the

45

Government in exile. As oppression increased in 1962, 100 to 200,000 of his countrymen fled to adjoining countries. 20,000 remain today mostly in separate and distinct camps scattered throughout Nepal.

A Canadian from Vernon, near Vancouver in his mid 50's and an enthusiastic entrepreneur, Keith oversees a variety of Business as Mission projects, bringing both work and hope to the people in the camp. Tenzin, his manager of Rasillo is in his mid 20's. He's also goalkeeper for the Tibetan national football team (which doesn't officially exist) and is about to leave for a two week tour, playing firstly in Dharamsala and then on to Italy, Spain and the USA.

In the middle of rebuilding and refitting, they explain the process of peeling the oranges, apples and pineapples, placing them into a juicer; squeezing the pulp via hand press. This will soon be replaced by a hydraulic press. Tenzin took on the manager's duties in 2004, employing initially 30 over 2 shifts but now he has 18 employees with a 9-5 shift, 6 days per week. It's a short seasonal operation, with only 30 days each for the three main fruits juiced up. The hope, however is to establish all year round production with the importation of fruit concentrate from India which then can be bulked up. This year has been a bad year, "But we're here for the long haul", they tell me. The Government minimum wage is 4,700 rupees a month. Rasillo pay 6000.

They plan to set up a Tibetan cultural information centre and provide tours of the camp, highlighting Tibetan history and food. Work is almost complete on a six room hotel alongside a mini conference centre and Tibetan restaurant. Seed money has previously gone into a Motor Cycle repair shop, a Bookkeeping company, an Electrical Repair shop, and an Animal and Vegetable (but no mineral) business which could be the basis of a Saturday market. They give seed money for inventory and capital equipment but, "we don't give salaries or buy vehicles...we give mentoring in business practices and accounting...all leading towards a partnership in a businessperson's association...giving after the fact training." This is all Phase 1, the foundation being with Tibetans, whilst Phase 2 is aimed at Nepali business start ups and further linkages.

At the restaurant, Keith opens up more as to his rationale. It's all about giving hope in exile and trying to question the automatic notion that Tibetan culture is synonymous with Buddhism. "The Dalai Llama is now saying it's Ok for Tibetans to become Christians."

"So, your religion should not necessarily define your sense of nationality?", I ask (bit of an echo from back home there). Tibetan culture has historically been nomadic, craft based and with a strong monastic tradition, existing alongside a matriarchal culture. The camp chief is female. Now it has to adapt.

"They need vision and hope. We present the vision and if they buy into that, they get hope. With the older Tibetan community we show respect and this allows us to work with a younger generation... forcing further the split....you can be an authentic cultural Tibetan without having to be a Buddhist".

Keith plans to give it another ten years before returning to Vernon. There's no Hollywood celebrity endorsements round here, but in the absence of a light bulb popping press conference, the relaxed tones of Western Canada have expounded a practical but strategic vision for the creation of hope in the Tibetan Diaspora, combating the hopelessness expressed through endemic ecstasy use and heroin addiction in the camps. He's the sort of man with a convincing narrative that leaves one feeling tired just listening. This portion of the Tibetan exile is slowly transforming, taking from an array of cultures, using western technology and business practices to re shape the possibilities for a whole people group.

Taking a moment to look round the Tibetan Café with its room portraiture of Royal Blue Chelsea FC flag, allied with Jimi Hendrix and John Lennon photos, suddenly it's 1971 again in this Shangri La of the mind, and I'm silent with privilege at being in the same London

47

bar as Alan Hudson and others from the Chelsea first team (I was an underage drinker) with 'Electric Ladyland' and 'Imagine', the soundtracks of youth. Time collapses in this suburban portion of the global village, to the accompaniment of a thousand rushing images, feelings and connections swirling past 'this falling man', reminding him that we are linked, not merely by the external symbols and icons of common cultural expression, but much more by the hopes, dreams and losses that define the communal over the solo nature of our journey, revealed in occasional flash points of recognition or resonance. These images and icons suddenly connect to the hidden world within, summing up a world of passion, hopes and dreams - a coming of age, where life was so intense and rich that you could taste it in the very air, and you've let that slip away in the mundane. That's the power of an icon... be they religious or secular: to sum up so much compressed emotion; to be a touchstone for its release and a place of gathering, where we're not so completely alone, with Lennon and Hendrix representing anger, angst, pain and loss. For a later generation it was Kurt Cobain, and now the clock's been wound back to the 70's again in this place.

I shake off this reverie in time to see a Rasillo van entering the camp whilst a Buddhist Monk strolls aimlessly by; the old and new Tibet co-exist in one frame. Tibet is its people, but a people without a land, who may yet decide to create a home, but only if they cease the limbo of waiting for The Return. The Al Awda of the Palestinians offers little comfort or prospect of that occurrence. I'm afraid I'll have to bookend this with a bit of 1969 lyricabelia, because even though "You can't always get what you want, but if you try sometimes...you just might find...you get what you need."

Finishing off our visit to Rasillo, we hear more about the Buddhist Temple on the hill. It has 60 monks there at any one time but 300 associates who are travelling light. Surrounded by a mass of prayer flags, it has to endure the indignity of Keith administering baptisms in the river flowing past the rear of the temple. I manage to turn too quickly from my gaze and walk straight into the top of the walk-through gate leading to some offices. Everything clunks and grinds just above the receding hairline. I also Let it Bleed...a little. I came from NI to Nepal but there's no A&E. I am offered an antiseptic gel, mostly alcohol, which will sting. I ask if I can drink some of it first, like in all good westerns? Request denied. Gel is applied, along with some tissues and hat to cover embarrassment. Keith reveals his balding pate, scored through his own encounters with low flying door frames. "After the third time, you learn to stoop", he says. I comfort myself with the fact that this is the second such collision. One more and I'm there, safe in the Clubhouse. We both mourn the loss of our hair a little, he possessing a tie back pony tail on his last tour in Nepal in the 90's, me with a memory of 70's weekend hippydom; he with remaining ear ring, me with a tissue under my hat.

We take our leave of the aid station and drive off past a lorry parked in homage to that scene out of The Italian Job, only this one is teetering over a paddy field and I wonder at the reach of Roman Abramovich; right into the Tibetan Refugee Camp on the outskirts of Pokhara. Who says money doesn't go a long way anymore?

1pm Paulas

On to visit Paulas Panday at the YWAM building, up past the bat cave. Paulas produces short radio dramas and biblical teaching programmes, sends them off to HCJB broadcasting from Australia back into Asia via short wave. His listenership is in the region of 20,000. This is a bit of his story.

He was born in 1979, in the small rural town of Burtibang, (Philip and Deborah lived in Burtibang in 1991 working with INF) into a Bhramin Hindu family with a strong adherence to religious ritual. At the age of 10 greater democracy was arriving in Nepal, along with old style Maoist communism with a little bit of Pol Pot seasoning. At 12, he became the chairman of the children's committee of the Young Communist group and then began to question communism as well as everything else, in part caused by interaction with some people from INF who didn't seem to conform to the stereotype of Imperialists. Friendships developed. He then stole a Bible to read up. Why? The Maoist language may have been one of helping the poor he says, but the practice was often very different with cronyism, elitism and corruption rife.

Serious illness hit him at age 14 with a dysentery that continued for three weeks without any relief. Herbs were administered and witch doctors called but without any improvement. On the 21st day of his illness, he felt he was going to die and was filled with fear. He remembers asking Jesus to save him and heal him. The next morning he was better and mobile. Then a few months later in another sort of test during a period of heavy rain, he prayed that the rain would stop. It did. At that point he committed himself to follow this Jesus. "So, from being a disciple of Marxism/Leninism, I then transferred at 14 to following Christ and wanted to be baptised." Some Christians from Pokhara obliged but this caused persecution and ostracism on a couple of fronts.

Firstly, the Maoists portrayed foreigners as exploitative people which any self respecting Nepali should avoid. The party line is: "They see something here that they want to steal...we don't know what it is yet but it must be something really important." This is a neat little closed circle of the political correctness of suspecting foreigners and thence, suspicion by association. Of course we do have the less than proud history of an export model of the robber barons of Imperialism dressed in the odd fig leaf of Christian Mission. Perhaps it was the particularly virulent bugs in the water which the Imperialists were after, which they were then going to force inject into obese westerners - bacterial diarrhoea as the new Slim Fast Rapid Reduction diet!

Secondly and more crucially, Paulas explains, "In our culture, if you say Christ is the only way, then you are outside the fold. Hindus can accept you as a Communist, even as a Christian, as long as you follow the Hindu rituals and observe festivals and events. But if you say Jesus is the one God, then you're rejecting the whole community." His relatives were insulted, scolded and his immediate family was given an ultimatum: "You will be abandoned by the wider family unless you disown him or he comes back to the fold. He needs to leave home or leave his new faith." His father/mother described him in a letter thus: "You're like an egg that's been dropped from this family and smashed and needs cleared away."

The cost of discipleship here began to be paid when at 15 he decided to leave home and go to Pokhara, managing eventually to get on a YWAM discipleship training programme and working with a Christian organisation for four years before moving into mass media radio communication. Over the years, as his family saw the genuine nature of his commitment, relationships were gradually mended. "Now my family is happy with me and there's a good connection."

In 2002, his father wrote to him, "You are the best child we have ever had".

"I was living a good life; they saw that, and not just following the foreigners for a good job or advancement."

Plans abound and in the future he hopes to complete an MSc in Sociology in Effective Communication for Social Transformation. Radio, he explains, "is still the best medium for transformation, available in the remotest of locations. It's also effective for Nepalis living throughout the Middle East, coming under pressure to convert to Islam. Many have written in to me for New Testaments." Personal change is also afoot, recently engaged to an American lady he met on a YWAM course. In fact she is due into Pokhara that very afternoon. Hence, our time is up and we have to move on.

Overall is the realisation that you pay a heavy price here when you get baptised. That's the point when you are seen as separating yourself from the dominant culture and the cost quickly starts to mount. With Paulas, the road hasn't been smooth but one can only admire his passion and commitment. You can be a Hindu and a

Christian and a Communist, that's all acceptable, but don't try to overturn the moneychangers in the temple, dependent on the dominance of the Hindu pantheon of gods, goddesses and rituals, in a place where religion and community are totally fused. I wonder if that happens anywhere else on the very western edge of Europe?

3:30 Chunman and the Street Kids:

McMillan is working me hard but I plead a mixture of nausea, lump on head and nothing since 8am as the necessary excuse in order to draw breath and grapple with flies at the German Bakery for possession of some Uber 'Grade A' sandwiches, before our next meeting. He only allows half a lunch hour and then we meet up with Chunman Harijan just before 4:00 in the frantic retail chaos at the Chipla Dunga (slippery rock) roundabout. The sun burns on and the traffic increases. Perhaps it's clocking out time, but not for some. He and his wife clocked in here at 9:30 to work with the street children. About 5 feet 4 inches and bursting with eagerness in tracksuit and cap, he's a part of the Nayagaun church on the south side of Pokhara and was previously a language teacher with INF; a father of 3 children, 1 boy and 2 girls, 15, 13 and 7 respectively. With his wife Ashka (Abraham Khan's sister - you'll meet him later), he's involved with feeding and befriending the street children who mill round the giant Bus Park. Their backgrounds vary; some are classic orphans, others runaways. Perhaps the father has found another wife and they are surplus to requirements. Some are Pokhara born and others come in from the hills to congregate with likeminded round the Bus Park.

For the last nine months they have led a team of four who prepare a daily meal of Dal Bhat for between 15 and 30, served up between 12:30 and 2:00 each day. It's the only meal these kids will get in a 24 hour period, which sort of explains why they eat five times more rice than others. It costs about 2000 rupees (£20) per day to feed 15 children.

52

Of course all this didn't just suddenly happen one day. For three years he visited the area every Thursday to build relationships. No short termism here. Kids on the street are seen as 'bad sinners' by the locals, as they have dropped through the family net which is just everything here. Because of that he explains, "they need ten times more love than others." Ostracised and denied property rentals once on the street, it's more than difficult to get off it. They survive by begging, stealing or collecting plastic bags to sell, to buy the glue or other substances with which they wrap themselves in a protective barrier of denial.

Chunman has a title for all the aspects of his work: Child, Youth, and Young Adult Activation programmes. It's sort of obvious but in case I hadn't deduced it, he endearingly tells me, "This is a loving and caring ministry." As well as providing food, he visits and encourages, telling Bible stories and telling his story. Along with Keith and Paulas, Chunman too is a man with a vision and a programme: to create hope, and a hope that could be actualised in a hostel, life skills or small business training, which would provide a way out and a way forward. He recounts how one street kid who lived with them for months eventually stole any money they had saved… "But we still have a weight in our heart for them…even though they steal from us. Their heart is very broken. We pray more for them and have a vision of them being transformed one by one."

An inspired Author having reached Ghandruk   Sungeeta, Anu Guest House, Dampus

Ghandruk

Purna demonstrating a Gobor Gas unit   Peaceful Guesthouse, Landruk

Annapurna mountain view from Ghandruk

View of Fishtail mountain from Ghandruk

Sellers and Porters on the trail

Mrs Khali Karki, Women's Skills Development   Keith and Tenzin,

Paulas   Abraham and Komala

Chunman and Ashka   Arbin and Bimila

56

Beauty for Ashes   Easter Sunday Marchers

My Hosts, Philip and Deborah McMillan   Faith Works

Distilling Essential Oil   Grace Church, Kathmandu

Though Chunman was born a member of the Harijan caste (a low caste), he's an elder in his church. It's the counter culture in operation, classically expressed in this unfashionable passion - this long term commitment with little easy reward, relentlessly reaching out to kids who have internalised layers of rejection, hardening themselves against others in their narrow but deadly daily battle for survival. In the Tibetan camp and here, we witnessed what is effectively the physiotherapy of the soul - stretching, pulling and enlarging, where what's shrivelled and atrophied is coaxed back into life. Without any expectations, love is poured into open wounds. And who knows, sometimes even these wounds close over. We say goodbye and they go back to work.

Back on the roof terrace of Sacred Garden, its 6:10pm and the sun has just set behind the hills, giving off that familiar warm glow merging into rust as the eye scans down the ridge line. Tee shirt and egrets, while 25cm of snow has fallen in some parts back home. It's been a day of busyness, of walking on the holy ground that is the lives of those on the journey...a journey outwards of service to others, touching the chasm of need but also a journey inwards, of connection, emotion and dreams. What's the difference between dreams and vision? The still small steps, without grandeur or announcing fanfare; the recurring walk into dark places, where those who stumble alone, are for even a few seconds or minutes, somehow connected with words embodied in flesh and bone. At some moment of transition, armchair debates have been abandoned for dirty messy thinking and feeling action.

From food prep to business plans, from heavy hearts to seed capital, from a prayer to action, from silence to airwaves, this is a day for remembering and honouring those working and resisting behind enemy lines, disrupting chaos with pockets of order, laying down payments for a different kind of future.

In the Tibetan camp, Keith looks for the small steps, where if you see even just one tiny bit of success, "You gotta jump all over it ...and make a real noise over it…otherwise you'd go mad". Paulas visions new broadcasts and races off to the tourist bus to greet his American fiancée, continuing their walk towards the aisle. Chunman and Ashka merge back into the crowd, baseball hat and chat and hands that cook and carry; the his and hers of the Angels of the Bus Park.

An hour earlier we had returned to the guest house to warm shower and the sound of bubbling conversation on the roof terrace. I hit my head as I step up into a new shower room and breathe a sigh of relief that that's the third time and I've learnt to stoop. I hit it again on the way out. You just can't trust the power of three.

Day 8

The Egret's shrill,/Jacob Zuma/ Returning Road/ Jam/,

KISC/ Americana/ Electricity and Water,/Mosquito Squadron

7am and the water carriers line begins. Red, green and white painted circles round the lakeside trees proclaim the independent republic of Bob Marley in the Himalaya. Volleyball is well under way in the park and footballers limber up; just another early morning start in order to squeeze the max out of the day. The brushing out begins all along the shop fronts and I return to the roof terrace where Machhapuchhare and Annapurna are visible this last morning in Pokhara. With more than a hint of regret, I leave the mountains and their still silence to return to the bustle of Kathmandu. But first the road back. Somehow I shall nod more vigorously to the prayer for protection and travelling mercies this time, as we move away from the protective watch of the mountains, under whose gaze I've learnt how to stoop.

A quick retail expedition to buy a winter jacket leads to a retailer who won't budge at all on his prices, the reason being, "I have 32 children." "Impressive", I think, even by Jacob Zuma standards. Then he clarifies that he helps support these children in the Rainbow Children's Home with 10% of his income. I relent and ethically purchase but see a cheaper one two minutes later.

We head off at about 8:30am and on the way back to Kathmandu we make great time. I'd forgotten the first 30km of corrugated tarmac, then two hours of the lushest beauty I've ever seen with green dense forests, paddy rice fields and river views complete with dotted rafting. We meet Catherine at stop off for soup, chips and coconut dunking biscuits. Her husband had been Philip's boss a few years ago. I ask how the relationship had been. "He was 200 Km away...it worked well", I am told.

We resume, having completed two thirds of the journey, but it's another two hours to Dodge. The winding ascent proper begins about 30 minutes later. "Driving isn't a game!" it wrongly says on the back of a lorry. It is here; one long game of chicken.

At one point we skirt a tight bend, with drop to ravine on the left and 30 metres later, a ravine on the right, a deadly distortion of the equal and opposite rule and move further on this long and winding road traversing ruts, ramps and holes in the earth's crust. Shortly after this, as we are on the inside track of our Olympian ascent, a White Mini Van Man fills the centre right portion of the road. A van behind and bus in front grants us no room for manoeuvre. If an oncoming lorry rounds the next bend, Van Man would get cosy with us and we might be forced off the track and lose any chance of a medal, tumbling into the ravine, failing to pass go and not collecting 5000 rupees. It was all rather "Disconcerting", as Tom Hanks observes in Saving Private Ryan, after receiving an update that "The Statue of Liberty is Kaput." White van edges ahead and our moment of crisis is averted...until the next one.

Looking back down the valley, some grimy miners emerge from the pit shaft, trudge into the green and off home for leek soup... (sorry, wrong film). It's more like 'Cast a Long Shadow', with a 1948 Kirk Douglas presiding over a massive 'Burma Road' type heroic relief effort of besieged Jerusalem; by hook or by trook. "Is this road ever quiet?" I ask. "No, they bring in the heavy stuff at night on the articulated lorries." We finally emerge panting over the ridge and begin a descent into the slightly cooler breeze of Kathmandu, self congratulating on a 5.5 hour journey almost complete.

But then the traffic suddenly locks in both directions, with no routes off to the side, this being the only road in from the west. I am told (encouragingly) that it once took them 4.5 hours to get the 10km from here to home. The Auguries are not good; the black entrails of dieseled cloud are offered up for inspection, just like management consultants, charging to tell you what you already know. Slowly, police in face masks appear and start to unravel the tangled knots but an hour is spent in occasional crawl amidst diesel smoke, fumes and choking breath. Philip hails a passenger on a bus travelling in the opposite direction as to what is causing the hold up. "A jam", we are helpfully told. Sardines are more loosely packed than some of the passengers in the mini vans opposite; folded, spooning, and locked in a rigor borne of necessity.

Forced waiting produces 20 questions from me:

Q: Pop of Kathmandu? Ans: 1.5 - 2million

Q: When did the insurgency start? Ans: 1996

Q: Numbers killed? Ans: 15,000 out of 28 million (a tiny proportion though compared with NI's proportion of over 3000 from 1.5 million)

Q: When did the country open up to outsiders? Ans: 1952.

There are 5 main castes

Q: What does the Swastika everywhere mean? Ans: The Swastika relates to the Goddess of Education, from the same root Sar Swati...Education.

I see a Swastika and a Star of David on the back of the same truck. Strange alliances indeed!

The jam is eventually scraped off and we move, at first stutteringly and then more regularly. 40 minutes later we arrive back at the flat and a moment of consummation occurs round the hazelnut coffee altar, before plunging onto the Good Friday evening service at the International Church two hours hence.

Quiet friendly, peaceful Kathmandu International Study Centre (KISC), a school for children of the expatriate community, also hosts the international church and is a haven of calm from the still frantic streets. We are greeted by the new American Pastor's wife, Theresa. I've heard of her, she's a mother...and a saint. What follows is a quiet reflective meditation on the last seven statements of Christ on the cross, delivered by Rendell Day from Alabama, long time Pastor with Habitat for Humanity. Gentle and secure, he leads us safely through the statements with responses via hymn or silent reflection, ending with communion bread and wine. While the communion is passed round, just flute and violin duet impeccably on "In the Cross...in the cross, be my glory ever...till my ransomed soul shall find, rest beyond the river." I suppress a tear rising to my glass eye as, for a moment it felt like we were in an Americana revivalist tent meeting circa the 1860's, that also included on its hymn sheet, Tis a gift to be simple, Tis a gift to be free, and The Battle Hymn of the Republic. This is the heart of the great America, brought by Rendell; reverential, warm, reflective, not ostentatious, expansive, concerned with justice and mercy unconstrained; a slice of the mid west in central Nepal. We filter quietly outside before the conversation bubbles up all around the courtyard.

I chat to Bob McLeod who works in radio, briefly to Ellen Bender , who runs a micro business called Beauty for Ashes, and Doug, a square jawed Doctor in Charles Lindbergh mould, heading off to the far west in a matter of weeks to start work in a remote hospital. We stumble home by torchlight the 15 minutes it takes in a darkened city, whose life is put on hold for the next eight hours.

Why does the electricity not supply? In a country of mountains and river flows, why is it not a net exporter of Hydro Electric? The issues of water supply and power are of course inextricably linked. Kathmandu's on/off power switch isn't predictable, so people check their candles and look at the cards showing the rotas, or get the updates on the radio (when it can be plugged in of course) before trying to do most things that we associate with the modern world. The myriad hums of petrol generators try to address the emergency shortfall needs a little, but mostly indicate comparative wealth or social mobility or, another reason for jealousy.

The government, of course, plans to build more hydro electric stations. So while the Maoists blamed the previous governments and governmental corruption for not advancing the building of new power stations, they spent most of their 10 year campaign seeking to destroy what infrastructure there was. The Provisional IRA also had a high rate of attrition on industry and economy and of course facilitated much building renovation and clearance through the hefty application of fertiliser or semtex. In Northern Ireland however, we had a modern wealthy state that was able to pour enough treasure into rebuilding and modernisation as well as providing the much needed leisure centres that gave us a necessary diversion from rioting. TV was rubbish in the 1980's.

Back here the Asian Development Bank and a Japanese International bank have a plan to at least help with the water supply issue to Kathmandu, by seeking to divert some snow fed rivers through a 20 Km tunnel supply. In perhaps 4 years time, it will be complete, but shortages are due to last for at least the next 15 years with an estimated cost of a mere US $300 million to replace the current system with an efficient one.

Arriving back in the flat, Philip suspects mosquito infiltration and helpfully compounds the earlier lung damage suffered in the traffic jam with excessive fly spraying. We choke and splutter. Later I realise how badly bitten I was on legs, waist and arm and scan memory for origin of the assailant. I flick through my mental card index of suspects and stop at a buzzing insect dive bombing my left ear at lights out the previous evening. I rose and thought I swatted it. Obviously it had a mate, intent on revenge, which was duly extracted. Reddened pulsing 50p sized bites are shown to nurse for inspection. "Aah...a mosquito", Deborah observes, "that's what it was", and produces more cream.

"Will I get malaria?" I rather pathetically inquire.

I suppress the suddenly forming mental picture of a shaking, sweat lathered denouement to my hols, only to be told, "not here in Kathmandu ...but if you were in the southern flat-lands...that would be different."

"But you might get Japanese Encephalitis!" Philip helpfully interjects. "That's ok then", I say... "cause I got that jab."

After another coffee, I retire to scratch a little more. It's my Tenko. Then I notice for the first time, the earthquake whistle hung from the head of the bed. The voice of Tom again says, "Disconcerting". I agree...and this time we're both a bit more serious about it.

Handy Hint: When being dive bombed by a mosquito...check that you have cleared the area of all angry relatives based on vendetta. Close windows and apply netting. Do not confuse with David McCallum and Dinsdale Landon in 'Mosquito Squadron.' They're the good guys.

Day 9

Some Central Points: Information about the range and extent of what FONIC actually does on the ground/ Skype Home/ Lost/ Globalisation

On a number of occasions throughout my visit, I had tried to get a grasp of the range of projects and the details of everything Philip and Deborah seemed to pack into long days and evenings for FONIC.

Eventually I gleaned what is below, by relentless grilling of people who don't like to blow their own trumpet. At one stage I did have to put Philip in a wrist lock with half nelson to extract this information, but he's better now. It just shows how much can be accomplished by a small scale responsive organisation, who know how to:

1.   Network effectively and with a range of local and international funders and providers to

2.   Identify need and respond rapidly to support people of ethics and integrity who

3.   Won't get the wool pulled over their eyes by sharp practice...

4.   Provide a high degree of accountability and ethics on the ground,

5.   To be flexible in responding to needs that are brought to their attention, in a way that a larger organisation couldn't without the making of detailed business cases.

With more funding, this model could accomplish even more, in empowering local people of ability, initiative and drive.

In a final two hour grilling, I start to grasp the extent of what has and is being accomplished here, in depth as well as breadth. I had identified ten major areas of involvement. It grew then to 12, then 14 A & B, and finally 19, the miscellaneous category meeting individual needs, or situations rolling. Eventually I have to call a halt; even they are surprised at the extent and the numbers helped. Here's the list:

•   Supporting the 19 children in Grace Rescue Home for the last 5 years. (Major funder)

•   Supporting children through school (10 children currently) over the last 5 years; 47 children have been supported through their education.

•   Supporting pastors and church workers:

65

- Bhim, a pastor in the Terai, working with the Tharu people;
- Nico, in his training and as a conduit to direct funding to
- individuals in rural locations;
- Shyam, in one of the Kathmandu Grace Churches;
- The pastor of a remote church in Gorkha;
- Gul, in East Nepal;
- Anos, a Sherpa in East Nepal and church planter;
- Kiron and Pitanbur supported through Bible College and an MSSc in Theology in the Phillipines;
- Betty's local pastors & church workers;
- Mahema Essential Oils Project - to provide employment and resource local communities.
- More recently Fonic is supporting dynamic and innovative new ministries such as Abraham Khan, who works with the Sonaha people and ex slaves' Tharu villages in the western Terai. Over the last 5 years FONIC have resourced him with bicycles (to get teams to remote locations), blankets, woolly hats (people die in the sub zero winters there), films (the Jesus film) and teaching and training materials. Immediate and responsive support is given to new projects.
- Deborah's work with the Didi/Bhini local health care/Bible study initiative
- Philip's chaired monthly meetings of the Great Commission Companies, the Business as Mission Network
- Meeting individual cases of need: a Medical Assistance Fund has enabled recent treatment of burns cases; 2 destitute families are also being supported currently
- Dreams and Visions: to take the work of FONIC out beyond Kathmandu (only 17%Population live in Kathmandu)
- ·Family Support funding: up to 6 families at a time

- Child Support Scheme: in conjunction with NI Churches acting as a conduit for the provision of bedding, blankets, clothes and rice

- Providing nursing support for senior nurses re procedures and good practice in Lumjung Hospital in Bisi Sahar (7 hours drive, turning right at half way to Pokhara) where Deborah worked as a Nurse Educator.

- Administering special funds from foreign donors for specific families and individuals with whom they had a connection when in Nepal. These fund training for doctors, meet education costs and the provision of general family support

- Medical Support A: running Screening Camps, rather like a school nursing check, identifying early difficulties or symptoms re eyes, ears, limbs, lungs and skin infections; giving a general physical check up

- Medical Support B: meeting individual medical needs which people could not afford themselves, such as eye operations, stents, treating burns, operations and hospital bills (19 such interventions in the last couple of years)

- Yearly grant to Grace Church for Sunday School resources

- Partnerships with other providers such as Human Development Community Services (purchase of office and other furniture equipment for their new building); ongoing linkages with FEBA and International Nepal Fellowship.

- Providing seed money for small businesses such as a guest house in Kathmandu, a local butchers, vegetable cart etc

- And…….. miscellaneous!!!

Apart from that, they don't get up to much! In their spare time, they get together with other underachievers like the Gills and do things like ford wide rivers and leap over tall buildings. You get a lot of bang for your buck with FONIC!

In the afternoon, I Skype home to my daughter, Nicola, who is walking in Castlewellan Forest. It's raining slightly there, they got 'de damp' sent up by an ashen-faced Angela from Limerick and the west of the province got the snow. Not a bad deal! It's our worst winter in NI since 1963 (when a team of engineers had to be mountain rescued after three days, snowed into the Divis mountain sub station). Time seems to redial as we hear that 200 engineers are being flown in from England to help those still without power. I recall in 1963, helping to dig the path clear, being Wellington booted, duffle coated, balaclavad and with plastic bags over our heads with eyes holes torn, being forced marched out to attend school. Now of course this is recognised as the cruelty it was and schools are closed if even the Jacuzzi is down. "How was it, Dad?" I'm asked. "Is it what you expected?" Now it's my turn to be grilled.

"It's like Slum Dog Millionaire", I say, "but with more contrast. Narrow uneven streets and lanes, even in a wealthier part of town but 20 yards away, someone could be living in a shack. Cows form part of the traffic flow; in fact, there is no traffic protocol. Houses are often left with steel rods and girders emerging from the flat four cornered roofs, as another storey may be added later and in Nepal there is always another story, on every street. Great food, teeming markets, wonderful fresh eggs as everyone seems to have chickens, or goats, or cows, or aspires to."

I tell her the teeming bustle of Kathmandu contrasts utterly with the lush greens and rolling valleys where lodges cost 200 rupees for a bed. The Gurung food is superb; it's a place of great beauty but where the basics of subsistence are so time consuming in food prep, collecting water and washing and cleaning.

"Do you not wish you could be there for 3 weeks?"

"Yes", I say, "but I didn't know it was going to be so great!"

"Does it make you want to go back?" she asks.

After this I decide to take a walk down by the open ground and fields; down past where the women wash clothes and the kids just wash. Past the rising smells, down to the river and the de facto rubbish dumps. I've gone far enough and now start to wind my way back, suddenly in the midst of unfamiliar shops and works and stares. Wrong turn taken, leading to arrival of panic. No functioning mobile...no Nepali...unsure of exact address apart from Lalitpur (which is a whole suburb). I retrace further for another 5 minutes and gasp relief at a familiar poster, make another turn and I ascend again on the right path.

> Basic Advice - Get a mobile, enter host's number and write their address down.

In late afternoon, my mosquito donated limbs throb even more. So we search in the local dispensaries for some Piriton anti histamine and calamine lotion...for dabbing purposes. I think the last time I was all white was also about 1963. Friends back home have chicken pox children in their care. No doubt whitened bodies there also struggle not to scratch. So from Kathmandu to Belfast, the cooling balm of calamine is applied. That's globalisation for you!

Day 10

From a Whisper to a Shout/ Easter Sunday March/ Betty La/
Eileen Lodge/ Durbar Square/ The Monarchy/ Grace
Rescue Home/ Mahema/ Little Ulsterisms

Easter Sunday morning, quiet and still; Mary in the garden in the cool
of the day. A whispered name, "Don't you recognise me?" That
whisper still echoes, in a conspiracy of hope, from when it began to
where it ripples out. Apparently that's what drives people out of their
comfort zones, to places like Kathmandu and beyond. It's evidenced
here in the lives of the people I'm privileged to call my friends and in
so many others like them, spread out with those ripples, bearing the
counter culture of allegiance to another king, way above any Lama
creed or nation.

Hymn singing drifts in at 5:30am; an alternative dawn chorus. At
Winston Churchill's funeral, after the benediction, a bugler high in the
dome of St Paul's Cathedral played the Last Post. Next, another
bugler placed on the opposite side of the dome played Reveille: "It's
time to get up, it's time to get up. It's time to get up in the morning."

Some who got up really early this morning were the marchers, very
different to our Ghandruk parade. At 7:30am we head off to see the
Nepali churches march. Driving up the lane we see a mother slap
the older of two boys round the ear. Apparently slapping occurs
mostly round the ear here. Along with untreated infections, perhaps
that's why there are so many Nepalis with hearing difficulties. It
wasn't a real clip round the ear of course; you need to come to
Belfast for that! 'What's that', you say? 'Your Power Cuts Tonight'
channel tells us that it's 6 pm to midnight tonight; a relative
improvement over the 16 hours a day of last year.

Developing Freedom and the changing face of "Mission.":
At 7:47am, we arrive at Pulchowk and tuck in to watch part of the

south side parade. Prior to the 1990 Constitution which officially guaranteed religious freedom, Christians could hardly pop their heads up above the parapet. According to the 2001 census figures, Christians were only 0.5% of the population but that probably was an under representation by an overtly Hindu state. The declaration of a secular state in 2008 ironically may broaden religious freedom. Overt proselytising is still frowned upon and western based mission societies no longer can be front line providers of education, health or community development services. That has to be carried out by local, Nepali based and staffed organisations. INF (worldwide) is differentiated from INF (Nepal). The role of Western Mission therefore has changed, from one of sending church workers to that of resourcing and empowering local initiatives.

So, from a face that was usually white, and hidden, that face is now of a different skin tone and very obviously on display.

Now look at this formerly barely acknowledged or tolerated religious grouping: banners displaying headlines such as "Jesus is our Hope", guitars and resurrection Tabla; a new marching trend with greens, blues, reds, and occasional face masks as two by two they march, the demographic overwhelmingly one of under 30. It'll be interesting to see the results of the 2011 census re religious affiliation. This is a transmission of real hope to a whole swathe of young people and now many are holding up signs in English. The crowd swells and thickens up to 5, 6, 7 deep, clapping, singing and dancing. Gratifyingly, even the government car has to wait for a gap in the ranks before crossing. Normally parades here are full of aggression and anger, heralding further conflict and confrontation. This is a different mood, with the only police needed today being traffic police. Most marchers have taken a half day or whole day's holiday to be here as Saturday is their day off. Fifteen minutes have suddenly passed and still they come, handing out flyers; these little messages of mercy. One group walks twenty paces, then does a Mexican Jump and repeats it in waves, stretching off into the polluted morning misty haze.

71

The palpable excitement is arcing across, impossible to ignore, and in ungainly homage to Zacchaeus, I climb up onto railings to get a better view. In a country where choosing to walk in the shoes of the carpenter can exert a drastic price with family and community, this is a stunning display of counter cultural allegiance. Three young guys given a booklet mentally scratch their heads as to what this is all about. Genuinely baffled looks abound.

Then another church converges from our right and flows ahead. Twenty minutes have passed now and it quietens, leaving you longing for the buzz of excited joy. You can't help but grin and then cry at their broad smiles, evidencing more than symbolically that they really are on the move and their day is indeed coming. On they march to the city centre to converge in Ratna Park - 20,000 of them, according to the press, stating their claim that they belong here too, from every caste, from every people group, with the same rights to expression as the Hindus or the Maoists or the traditions and weight of the dead generations; convinced they've met someone, and looking on from the bleachers, I'm convinced I've met someone too, on the way to a different kind of smog shrouded Emmaus. From 8 years of age to 60, they've told a story, sometimes with words and songs, but mostly with smiles, that there is a future, there is a hope; it's shimmering under their skin and escaping out through their eyes.

On the way back, we see a street Palm Reader with only one taker. Business is slow on Easter Sunday morning. We then drive past two Buddhist monks and I want to ask if they like chips, because then they could moonlight as Chipmonks and I wonder what they'd make of Monkstown in North Belfast! We stop by a stall just round the corner from the flat and Philip hails a lady called Betty La, not related to Anna Lo (The Northern Ireland Assembly's only ethnic member) and not from Annalong (little town in the south of County Down)! Betty helped set up one of the first Tibetan churches in Nepal and doesn't possess a traditionalist theology, I'm told. I find my interest in Betty rising. She apparently finds it hard to read the Bible, gets tired and says to God, "Please speak to me in the normal way", which for her is in dreams. The local Tibetan church hadn't joined in on the march; again a self imposed cultural separation. I suppose it's some way of cherishing "home." To share in the locale would perhaps somehow dilute the power of its memory. Yet, there is a home; she was born here. The deification of exile prevents the very building of the new, in the here and now that they so badly need.

More snapshots: 1000 a day here, like the man on his pushbike, with the metre round tin bowl worn on his head like some gigantic pith helmet or extra from the Imperial Cruiser on Star Wars. Another crazy load was carried by the man with the massive box panniers and tie ons either side of his bike, the load swamping him and the bike. Gaining movement at all was a triumph against the forces of gravity.

Arriving at 10:30 this Easter Sunday morning at the International Church, it's unsurprisingly full. Eileen Lodge sits in wheelchair at the end of the row, her involvement with nursing dating back to 1954. She only built two hospitals and took out Nepali citizenship, driven by an all consuming call to work with leprosy sufferers - a shining example of the proud tradition of the church serving the weakest in society, punching way above its numerical weight in this society. Now in her 80s, she's been struck down by dementia, but she's at home here, dignified by the respect of all around her. The sermon is a classic in the intentional dropping of G's. It may not be the Queen's English as we all know and speak it in Surrey but, "It's Friday but Sunday's Comin" echoes out in call and response. It's an Alabama shortening but not bread.

Sunday lunch in the tourist spot of central Patan, which along with Bhaktapur, are the other ancient cities that have merged with the third member of the triumvirate, in what is now known to the outside world as Kathmandu. It's an assault on the senses, these narrow teeming retailed streets with layers of local and international fashioned shoes, clothes, bags and accessories. We sneak past the security guard collection point for tourist extortion while Deborah explains we are locals, then crouch and wind our way up the narrow stairs to the roof of the Café de Temple overlooking Durbar Square, part of the old walled city (or if it wasn't, it should have been) where homage is evoked for Jackie Pullinger by that realisation, who really must take much of the blame for an upstart Bedeshi visitor.

Taking our leave and being worked hard, even on a Sunday, we drive through the centre en route to Grace Rescue Home and the Mahema Building. Not far from Ratna Park is the Royal Palace where a cull of family members took place on 1st June 2001. Crown Prince Dipendra allegedly shot dead his parents, King Birendra and Queen Asiwari, a further 8 other princes and princesses and wounded 5 others before shooting himself. The King's brother, Gyanendra just happened to be 200 kms away in Pokhara and had the greatness he perhaps felt he was born for, thrust upon him. The official report didn't completely dampen theories of conspiracy. One royal sister survived. She suffered further injury when her brakes failed two weeks later and limousine hit a wall. Then her helicopter lost all power and dropped like a stone just as it was flying over the deepest lake in Nepal. Her middle name wasn't lucky!

Needless to say, the already less than popular monarchy, which had dissolved parliament and assumed absolute power during the Maoist insurgency, never really recovered. In April 2006, weeks of mass protests, led to peace negotiations, a peace accord in November that year and an interim constitution. Fresh elections in 2008 saw the new assembly declare a federal democratic republic and the abolition of the monarchy. It was the top item on its agenda.

The first tarmac road in Nepal was constructed just outside the Palace in Durbar Marg. The King had a Mercedes carried up in pieces from India and thence constructed on site. He was then able to have the royal saloon driven up and down the 1000m or so of Durbar Marg road, as you did, in the days of the God King. It got him out of the house. There isn't a tremendous groundswell of popular demand for the return of the monarchy.

74

Grace Rescue Home

A place where the history holds more hope is Grace Rescue Home, which has been in its premises since 2006. The metal bunk beds, with their practical heavy duty frames have saved lives before, in other earthquake zones. FONIC has been the major supporter of the rescue home for the last 5 years, which cares for 19 children from a range of backgrounds - some orphaned, some abandoned, some suffering horrendous abuse or neglect. They've been brought together, given protection, education and the possibility of a future. The landlord now has demanded a doubling of the rent so all will have to be looked at afresh regarding the viability of a move or whether to redeploy some children with families from the church. Philip recently calculated that it is seven times more expensive for FONIC to support a child in the Rescue Home than a child in a family. Little wonder donor organisations are reluctant to support institutions. The house mother, Sita, had her Downs Syndrome child of 2.5 years die in her arms whilst waiting to be called in a hospital queue. The procedure here is to visit a hospital, get issued a number, which comes with a time and you then try to be down for that time. The child died waiting. Her husband later ran off with another woman and Sita was reduced to carrying cement and breaking stones. Now she's a proud housemother, committed to the welfare of these children, and she's been rescued too. We talk to some and hear about their progress in school and their dreams for the future. I'm conscious of not wanting them to feel on display so we don't impose for too long. But what is obvious is that real change to real lives has been transacted here. The future beckons with much less menace now.

Mahema Essential Oils.

We move on from the Rescue Home and down to the Mahema compound close by, where Philip and his partners have invested great amounts of time and energy into Mahema Industries. It's all about broadening and supplementing income for local small scale suppliers through building their capacity to generate a viable cash crop, perhaps for many, for the first time.

The process commences with the supply of Steam Distillation equipment to Village Development Committees (effectively small scale Farmers Co-ops). Government grants subsidise much of the purchase cost of about £3000 for the distillation kit. Philip explains that Essential Oils crops must be grown in a way that doesn't negatively affect existing agricultural production, as "we want to add to the overall income of a village, not merely rotate the means of how the income is generated."

Normal Agribusiness will go for replacement crops to the current subsistence model, saying you can earn X and buy your own food with the profits. The downside of this is that profits might be hived off by a few strong characters in the village, leaving the rest of the local population actually worse off. Mahema's big ideas are additionality, ethics, quality and provenance.

Each village may have a community forest they can access. Lemongrass may be growing naturally and perhaps sporadically harvested for tea or just ignored. "Mahema seeks to work in partnership with our producers. They sign a contractual agreement which states that Mahema will buy all that you will produce this year, at an agreed price (we will revisit the agreed price if it changes) and guarantee the quality of the product.

Mahema pays 1200 rupees a litre to the dealer for, say Lemongrass. They also advise the Farmers' Co-ops how to increase efficiencies, so they can boost their profit margin even more. Targeted at the Fair Trade type customer, they want someone who buys Mahema Essential Oils to know the ethics of the process: built on relationships that respect local producers, enabling an upward development that raises both local standards of living and the quality of that living. Mahema will then seek to evaluate that progress via an objective measurement tool such as the Human Development Index, which looks at levels of economic activity, health and educational opportunities, as well as typical earnings per family per month in US Dollars. The process above will provide the customer with a "story" and the provenance (re the origin or locale in which it was produced) of each batch will be evidenced through unique reference numbers, showing date and area.

There are currently six plants with approximately 1000 families within the Mahema production network. Philip obviously plans and hopes this network will expand further. The harvesting of Roselle for Tea production may add yet another option to the portfolio.

The detailed means of the production process can be found at the back of the manuscript…for all the nerdy engineers.

An evening follows of omelettes, breads and chocolates, the sort of evening where you hit a thirst zone and only cup after cup of tea will refresh. Mother's sayings, family histories, child raising tales and little Ulsterisms all tumble out until the time for their phone home. I retire to my room for a 15 minute lie down and wake to the post midnight silence broken only by the cramping of stomach and the tip toe to the bathroom.   It hasn't been a typical Sunday.

Tomorrow/today/Monday we are going to see Higher Ground Enterprises and many many others.

Day 11

Business as Mission, Top of the World/ Beauty for Ashes/ Faithworks/ Abraham Khan/ Higher Ground and Culturemix.

Business as Mission: **"Business is a Christian calling…providing economic, social and spiritual help to employees and nations."**
(Steve Rundle and Tom Steffen. Great Commission Companies. (2003)

I lie in bed really late, until almost 7:40am. I get up and no doubt there has been two hours work completed already. Impressively there has! Philip has got Deborah's laptop going again. It was the lead. Eventually bits of two bad leads were split together to make one good! It's another polarity switch in the mountain kingdom undoing the Chiles law of 2 good 2 bad. The alternative Nepali maths: 2 minuses equals a plus. A full day of visits lies ahead. Insert Imodium…no … I mean swallow!

Top of the World Coffee

On up past the crowd of day labourers on the ring road waiting for hire, our first stop is with Dale Nafziger of Top of the World coffee. I avoid greeting him with a top of the morning. Instead, after guard dog Rocky's welcome of barking and bared teeth, we are greeted by the richest, sweetest ever coffee aroma of vanilla and hazelnut. He imports from Ethiopia, Colombia and Thailand, as well as local Nepali coffees from a large farmers co-op.

Dale has been here for the last 25 years in one guise or another. Originally with a Mennonite mission, he worked in hydro power for 17 of those years and then spun off into the creation of small businesses, inspired by the Business as Mission model. Indeed, he is the inspiration behind the Business as Mission group, the Great Commission Company grouping of which Philip is chairman. Three operations keep the wheels turning for him: French Fries and Pizzas to local restaurants and in 2008, the Coffee. Married to his Darjeeling Nepali wife Bethsaba, they have two children, one adopted. Dale might indeed be a relative of Tom Smothers, Pennsylvanian, and speaking in a slow thoughtful drawl. Words are rationed, economical and utilised for descriptive precision, not small talk.

I ask if he could define the Business as Mission model and how it has worked in practice. Dale looks to Bethsaba, who defines it instead through story. She started the Fries business, hiring Raena, a low caste orthodox Hindu lady who, after two years working there, had the opportunity to observe a lifestyle. Then they talked more openly about faith/s and after that she wanted to be baptised and now is a leader in church along with her husband. Their two children also attend.

Bethsaba believes she was noting a lifestyle, seeing and hearing the simple expressions of love from a husband and how a father can be with his children, as opposed to her experience with her own heavy drinking father. Perhaps also the Christian God compared favourably with the capricious nature of the Hindu gods and goddesses. Raena was the first to come along to church. Then later she prayed for the healing of a local boy who was dying. He was healed and that family and their children now attend also. The boy's father is now their delivery driver.

Exciting stuff.. She's the dynamo alongside Dale's steady centre. "Is there anything you'd want to add?" I ask Dale.

"No," he replies. "That pretty much says it all." That's Business as Mission.

Rocky gets the Pizzas spoiled by the erratic power off system. This Italian stallion coulda been a contender but was spoiled by spoilt pizza. As we penetrate further into the building, towards the stores and blending area, the senses swirl in delirious ecstasy as the aural hit increases its intoxicating and addictive power. Pity none of us likes coffee! He roasts on demand and we demand some.

It's of course a seasonally affected disorder, peaking in November and December and tapering off through out the year. With the unpredictable spikes in electricity supply, voltage fluctuations can easily destroy machine control systems, so Dale runs his own 14 solar panel roof back up system supply when producing. It's an extra capital cost for business here, almost doubling the capital investment required. In the hallway, there's a framed presentation on 'The Faith of our Fathers'; a report on Dale's Father and his funeral. This rich dignified moral tradition in the American patchwork quilt is now modelled out in a far flung outpost which will be forever Mennonite.

We exit, laden with freshly ground coffees and go on past the Gurkha Pathfinders poster to track down our next victims, in the Beauty for Ashes workshop.

Beauty For Ashes (BFA)

After circling suspiciously round a major road, we eventually see a small black Beauty for Ashes sign with a white line drawing of graceful female with hands and head reaching upwards - Beauty for Ashes, dignity for shame; a bit more attractive than our own metal framed 40 feet high female icon on the Queen's Bridge, holding outstretched a large metal ring, symbolising 'The Harmony of Belfast'. AKA: the Thing with the Ring, or Nuala with the Hula.

Ellen Bender arrives just after us on her Honda scooter. She removes face mask and helmet to revel Robin Wright-Penn's young sister who has escaped the Holywood press pack to work under the radar in a socially useful enterprise, on the outskirts of the city. She's Californian and possesses an MSc in Applied Behavioural Analysis; applied via a stint of working with autistic kids and adults. During that time she took a YWAM Discipleship Training course in New Zealand where she effectively was bitten for mission.

Three and a half years ago she arrived here with a vision of helping women who have come out of sexual exploitation and trafficking or are at high risk of being drawn into it through working in 'cabin bars.' Ellen came up with the business model and initially started visiting recovery homes to seek to identify those ready to move on. Her first 3 employees were referred by SAATHI, a local Non Governmental Organisation. BFA has been in operation one and a half years, has 6 full time staff ranging from 15 years to 30+, as well as a local manager. Devotions occur between 9 and 10am each morning and

80

her staff are paid whether they attend or not. Though two are Christians, individual faith is not an issue in terms of recruitment; it's all about moving people forward and offering alternatives to those at risk of, or damaged by exploitation.

We are greeted by a hive of industry with threading, sewing and packaging all carried out in a basic room perhaps 12 metres by 5, with a display wall of designs for our perusal. Her American business partners look after the designs and she oversees the production and marketing. In the USA, they have sold $10,000 worth in the last 4 months, with a range that runs from $4 for ear rings to $40-50 for necklaces. The designs are both original and high quality, unlike many other businesses in Nepal where the word 'Copyright' usually translates into 'the right to copy.' Foot powered sewing machines create the presentation bags and pouches and at about 5000 rupees each to purchase, these modernised Singers from our working class folk memory are still a serviceable and appropriate technology, especially when the power goes off. The building they are in has capacity for real expansion and Ellen wants to see it get huge...because the need is huge. Another link in the Business as Mission chain.

We leave BFA and the motor bike in front is suddenly enveloped in the black smoke ink fumes of the giant lorry he's too closely tracking. It's an altitude alternative to the giant squid discharge in 20,000 Leagues Under the Sea. The air quality declines further and I feel like I've just had ten Woodbine. The last time I had a Woodbine, I had to lie down on the flower and raise my hand to request First Aid. No room in the Isuzu for that. I must mask up in my own version of Hurt Locker.

> Handy Hint: Dick Turpin may indeed have worn a mask...but you still need one too.

Faith Works

On to Faith Works, which is a handmade backpack small enterprise. A 4x4 stops traffic on the Jawalakal roundabout to answer his mobile phone call. I take his registration number and may report him to PSNI traffic branch when I get home; another three points in the city of a million points a day. A passing motorcyclist carries out his own mobile call with the local hands free kit; phone jammed up under his helmet against his ear, he swerves away from the jam.

Faith Works is now so busy, they are sub contracting. Surrendra knew a family that had sewing skills but no machines or product. Seeing a market for small trekker backpacks, he bought the machines, employed the family, and hey presto, quality products at reasonable prices, hopefully soon to be available online recast with a No Fat Cats logo. (No Fat Cats is the soon to be an online company and portal whereby one will be able to purchase from a range of Nepali and other small businesses products). He donates a proportion of the profits to support two children's homes in Kathmandu.

Needing some cash, I begin to grapple with the lines and the multiple layers of banking bureaucracy for 45minutes, eventually extracting more Rupees. The Western Union money transfer till line is even longer; testament to the growth of migrant labouring abroad and their transfers home. We escape just across the road to the Higher Ground Coffee Shop and an iced tea as cold as Alex is ingested. "Worth waiting for!"

Abraham Khan: The Running Man and the Ex Slaves

Abraham likes running. He was limping though when we met him outside the restaurant. He'd been running yesterday, chased by the Police at the Bagmati bridge, but they caught up with him because he pulled a muscle. He'd been handing out free copies of the Jesus DVD and had the temerity to give some to four officers in their van. Hence the chase; they wanted two more for their mates who were round the corner.

Glasses and jet black hair, lithe and lean in orange shirt and jeans, Abraham was born in 1974. His father was the first Muslim convert in Nepal and was brought up in Pokhara, his wife, Komila hailing from a valley just to the south. Abraham has a Law Degree, he used to play volley ball and of course, he runs. He works mostly with groups in the Terai, the flatlands of the South West and most recently has begun to work with the children of former slaves. This has been a multi generational process of bonded labour, in effect selling oneself to a local landowner, with a pledge to work his land in exchange for two meals a day. No wages, just long hours, and access to a shack, water, food and a plot, all owned by the landowner. Children and grandchildren are then born into this slavery, knowing no other lifestyle.

In 2006 the Government finally banned this practice, setting the bonded labourers free. Many didn't know what to do, conditioned as they were by generational bondage and some went back. Others coming out of slavery long ago also felt it was better back in Egypt! However, most are now in large camps of about 400 each in Tikapur West. Nepal Abraham had worked with the Sonaha people in this area, helping them to resettle and rebuild many homes there after flood damage. He was the means by which Samaritans Purse Ireland (soon to become Team Hope in Ireland) in partnership with FONIC Trust were able to rebuild and stock these villages with goats.

83

He was taken to these ex slave camps in April 2009 and began to work with them post October 2009. They're on government lands and have built very simple shacks from bamboo and mud (without broadband access), but the children are now at least attending school. They're mostly Tharu people, agricultural labourers practising an animistic Hinduistic but not a supercalafragilistic or expealidocious belief system!

Abraham had worked as a local organiser for the Southern Baptists until October 2009, when he left a high earning position to get a covered wagon and go west, despite their attempts to have him stay. He likes travelling light. Few other groups or organisations had ever worked with these people before. "Our strategy", he explains, "is to reach these people through their children, by story telling, showing films, buying and supplying pens and pencils and drawing books. My uncle's church in Tikapur West is 25 minutes away on a motorcycle and they have brought 6 families to Emmanuel Church and since then, another 5 families (with about 6 in each family) come to church. Now we go there each month." He'll use the small amount of money I am to pass on from home group to buy pencils, pens, notebooks and sweets. He gets a big audience, they colour in Christian books and he shares about the gospel. They also use "Bible verse memory programmes. A friend can memorise Bible verses and he has visited these camps where, along with guitar and drums, we sing and tell Bible stories."

Their favourite Bible story so far is "Jesus feeds the 5000," as they truly understand hunger. "My biggest dream in my life from this time forward is to work with these children. They have a staple diet of Chapati, which is just the cheapest bread, Roti very occasionally and need better nutrition. Even once a month would be good and we would have the opportunity to have a whole day with them, singing, telling stories, colouring in and playing games like pass the parcel, telling your story or your names and reciting verses. It would cost about £300 for one village to feed them for an all day event. There are 12 villages I'd love to repeat this with, and about 400 in each village." Deborah then mentions the idea of involving a local NGO in getting a week's training for Abraham and Komila in Nutritional

Education, to encourage the villagers to use local foods to enhance nutrition.

He has taught them to say grace and hopes maybe they'll say it at home, as "children can open up real channels of communication with their parents." He works with a team of 10 volunteers from Christian Children's Fellowship, whilst others from Emmanuel Church visit every week. His involvement is with the ex slavery kids, the Sonaha people, delivering discipleship training in the West, channelling medical care, showing the Jesus film and distribution of Bibles. He has an award from the Nepal Bible Society for distributing the most Bibles in 2008; 2009 is still being counted!

I enquire if he will take any time off and watch football this summer.

"I may take a couple of hours off to watch the World Cup and support Argentina."

"Ah well, nobody's perfect!" I think. Later that evening, Lionel Messi produces a mesmerising solo display, scoring all 4 goals which eject Arsenal from the Champion's League. What do I know?

Higher Ground.

Our time is up and we are due to meet Bimila of Higher Ground Enterprises at 3:00pm. She's another innovator.

It's never nice to be threatened. Many have had to live with it as a constant during our troubled times in Northern Ireland. The Civil War in Nepal threw up a multitude of similar experiences but since Peace was processed from 2006 onwards, there shouldn't be any cause for concern, should there?

Bimila Shrestha Pokharel is a member of the Great Commmssion Companies, Business as Mission group and the entrepreneur behind three small businesses: Higher Ground Coffee Shop, Bakery and Crafts business. She is married to Arbin and has 2 children aged 6 and 4.

She attended Calvin Seminary in the USA in 2000 to study medicine but following her conversion, she changed to a Social Science degree with a Business major. It was then that she met Arbin, the only other Nepali student there. Returning home, starting in her own kitchen, she began to train local women in baking skills.

In 2005, aspirations began to take on more concrete form with the purchase of a coffee shop and the launch of Higher Ground Café. This intentional statement of hope and optimism began recruiting those most in need of employment to support their families. Higher Ground Crafts came next. An employee mentioned she would love to make some jewellery and Bimila then supplied some materials and began experimenting with jewellery, getting feedback from networks of friends and starting to sell to house parties. The designs were popular and the business started to take off. Now they've begun to produce to order and hopefully expand even further. Clanrye Trading already has a relationship and hopes to buy and sell more of her product.

Higher Ground Bakery followed soon afterwards, with the same employment ethos. In April 2010, she had 22 employees; a few weeks later, people approached her and she expanded to 30 - from Micro Business to Small to Medium sized Enterprise! Further expansion rests on increasing sales and she has that vision for growth, especially the Crafts business expanding into the production of bags, fabrics, sewing and knitting. It's not about empire building, but meeting individual cases of need that come their way, providing that dignified employment so badly needed as well as encouraging creativity and hope amongst the younger girls.

In the future, she'd like to have not only crèche facilities, but also to be able to provide "a safe house, a community shelter. As we reach out and engage more and more with girls in the Dance Bars, we'll now need to focus on the whole family." Her idea, mentioned earlier, of setting up an NGO Training Centre that will train and up skill local women therefore has a strategic context.

It's not without its cost though as this is Business on the Frontline. As well as upsetting the stereotype that limits female entrepreneurs, she has also incurred the wrath of a violent Hindu extremist group, the Nepali Defence Army, the latest armed group seeking to raise its profile. On 26th May 2009, they set off a bomb 15 minutes into Saturday morning Mass in Assumption Roman Catholic Church, close to the bakery and crafts business. Father Bogati said, "We had received threats over the phone from this group about six months ago, but we took them lightly." Bimila's letter arrived soon afterwards, warning that she and the church/bakery were next. Her husband pastors their church which meets behind the bakery. To have a profile as a successful faith based business woman is to doubly enrage militant Hindu traditionalists. She hasn't even slowed down slightly!

The limiting cultural norms in Nepal are unpacked by Bimila, who outlines her wider motivating goals: "Higher Ground is about seeking to develop initiative...as even those with a Business Degree lack initiative." Explaining further: "The education system in Nepal is a rote learning system. It encourages a culture of deference and respect, imposing a sort of cultural straitjacket. No one challenges the fact that there's no electricity, or that the roads are so bad."

Philip pitches in with an analogy used to described Nepali culture to him. "Nepali Culture is like two crabs climbing up a rock. The second one catches onto the first and hangs on. As it climbs, it gets exhausted; then the second one pushes it off and continues." Individualism par excellence.

Slowly though, with a new culture emerging amongst the young, some of whom were seen on Easter Sunday morning, they're chipping away at this. However, Bimila acknowledges that there is still a problem of excessive deference, even in the church. But that's a rock on the road, not a roadblock for this Christian Businesswoman, part of the heart of this process of forging out a new culture of innovation that refuses the limitations of inherited local norms and patriarchy.

Her ultimate goal is to help local churches to grow but this can only occur through a myriad of individual stories and then family linkages. For her, business is the vehicle through which those changes can happen. Like with Top of the World Coffee, stories bubble out: "One of our cleaners at the café felt so down and oppressed by her background of Animistic Buddhism that we asked if we could pray over her. After that, her husband, two children and her relatives saw such a change in her that they asked to be baptised. Seven families ended up being affected by this." More and more they find themselves working with girls in or in danger of being drawn into the sex trade. As with Beauty for Ashes, business expansion means enablement to meet need.

These new entrepreneurs, these businesses on the frontline are engaged not only in challenging cultural and business norms, but much more significantly, in challenging despair itself through an emerging network, a Conspiracy of Hope.

It's worth putting in some recent Facebook posts in June this year as to the developing story.

> *Higher Ground-Kathmandu, Nepal has been praying, waiting and exploring ideas for last 5 years how we can get involved more with community development through Higher Ground...and finally we are moving towards registeration of small NGO in Nepal .....pray for this process .*

> *Pray for us today as we are going to the government office to register a small Non-profit through which we can do effective and sustainable community development service in the villages helping women, youth and children at risk through skill development training, informal/formal education,*

health camps, micro-enterprise...s opportunities for women, rescue of women and children if they are at risk!

We are now preparing two rooms for shelter homes for the women at risk and other two rooms for day care centre/play group for the little ones! It is never boring at Higher Ground, new things are happening as the needs arise!

Who can fathom the government system in Nepal? It has been frustrating doing back and forth from one office room to another, and one floor to another and one office to another.......it is the story of a very disorganized and corrupt system here.....

We are on the process of starting small microenterprises in two different villages one in Thankot and another one in Lumjung...

Cultural Hint: Animistic Buddhism is different from Animated Buddhism, cause that would be an ADHD cartoon monk.

7:30 Cullturmix.   A Norwegian Connection

Finally, after some refuelling, on to see the Norwegian choir that evening (perhaps a Saga Holidays sponsored event). It's in the most impressive building I've seen in Kathmandu. It's the St Xavier's Jesuit School where local traditional musicians will merge their flutes, drums, tables, harmonium and Sarangees (the local vertically played violin) with Norwegian vocal power. Reports that they arrived in a fjord transit were untrue.

They are fronted by a giant I'll call Olaf, who has an immaculately groomed, Santa-like, straightened 9 inch wide beard that shimmers and flows in rippling waves of light grey, ending just above his navel. This provokes debate amongst us on the mechanics of soup eating and whether he has a beard bag for soup or spaghetti. However, if he really liked both of these, he could consider combination eating of

89

some pasta soup....to limit the mess.

He introduces and expounds on the virtues of 'Cullturmix', where differing cultures are placed together and forced to learn from each other during a shared enterprise. Learning, love, peace and understanding are thence encouraged. That's the theory. So, back in Northern Ireland we were wasting our time all those years hammering out a Consociationalist solution involving PR, D'Hondt and Cross Community voting safeguards, when what we really needed were more choirs. The Donaghadee Male Voice Choir I know certainly did their bit but obviously they were merely voices crying out in the wilderness. Don't think there were enough Norwegian Choirs up in the hill country during the Maoist insurgency either.

This choir had a preponderant number of women in it who looked rather severe whilst the minority male contingent may have been re commissioned from former Eurovision entries, because it really is, in true Beach Boys lyric style, "Three girls for every boy." It's not an overly attractive ratio and certainly doesn't presage another summer of love. I suspect some males may have been drugged. One Manchurian Candidate signals heightened emotive involvement through slight shoulder shift.

Olaf informs us that American Gospel music is big in Norway. I begin to shift uneasily in my seat. We are encouraged to "Shut de door...Keep out De Debil...Keep de Debil in de Night". The devil of illiteracy, bad spelling and the stereotyping of black Afro American culture perhaps wasn't in mind re the choice of material, but fortunately there was no one there who could be directly offended. I looked round.

However, there were plenty of Nepalis who could have been offended in pre performance practice when one of the Nepali groups, with a rather soft voiced 15 year old girl singer, was struggling to be heard over Olaf's rather insensitive strident conversations with his choral colleagues. People shushed a lot but with little effect. More intense but wasted shushing continued. This was no Oslo accord! Seemingly oblivious to the discourtesy, and unaware that this developing international incident could involve the drawing of the Gurkha knife, the Khukri (which cannot then be sheathed without blood being drawn) and a quick filleting of said Norwegian, I began to see the headlines loom: 'Norwegian slain at Peace Concert.' Helpfully, I decide to bring some Belfast Peace Process etiquette to the table. It does however take the form of an oral advisory diplomatic declaratory statement from a nodding head of disagreement, along the lines of "Tell Olaf to Shut it!" It appears to reach his ears and have the desired effect. It was another victory for the Peace Process abroad; one of our few viable exports. Just bring us to your tired, your troubled masses et al and we'll write up another Peace 3 proposal!

I digress. Back to 'Shut de door'. Larry Grayson didn't shut the back door and look what happened to him. We are then informed in call and response:

"When I was a little baybee".....(It was hard to imagine Olaf ever having been a baby)... "Shut de door...keep out de debil..."

"And My Mama used to tell me...Shut de door..." (presumably she was extremely hairy too...but I hoped she shaved!).

She also must have passed on all sorts of Volk knowledge because we were then given active learning instruction on how to milk cows and play the Veeolynn (not Vera Lynn, as we'll never meet...and I don't wax!) during singing of said songs of the fjords. I confess I was still a bit angry somewhere about the sacking of Bangor Abbey by the Vikings in 824, but we've got to move on I suppose!

The concert takes a completely unexpected turn with the two Sarangee players soloing with Danny Boy (not the London/Derry Aire as there are harmony issues with that stroke in the city). We beam and the other musicians merge and move into a long lengthy

91

crescendo with lots of drumming again; strange familiar ground here. The evening ends with joint massed choirs, intertwining folk melodies, rhythms and instruments which at last work and we applaud, but also feel relief at having avoided bloodshed on another night out in Kathmandu. I'll have to wait for the Irish bar for that!

Day 12

Priyanka and the Rubbish Man/ HDCS/ ABBS/ Mark Gill/, Thamel,/ Kilroys and the Bhagmati

My birthday. Another year turned, another year closer to the choice of Care Home. Kathmandu lung has started to set in and I wheeze a bit in requisite fashion, perhaps hastening that process. It's Good Day Sunshine on the iPlod and just before 6am, I decide to walk the 40 minutes up the ring road to photograph the crowds of day labourers waiting for work. Two girls in Bangor Academy blue uniform are on their way to school. A very small man clambers up the side of a very large skip to deposit his collected rubbish. Up past the prayer flags of the Tibetan Refugee camp, school buses arrive and depart. Sellers open bike and mobile shops and newspapers have long been on display. The tallest schoolboy ever lopes in John Cleese silly walk style, running for his bus. Three ladies pass with full loads of vegetation on their backs and a boy in Tae Kwan Do kit is on his way to his morning lesson, or perhaps more likely returning.

The air is cooler; one could almost be back in the mountains again, until I hit the ring road proper a bit further up. The motor rhythm heartbeat of this city quickens into full swing with black smoke exhaust fumes building again and merging into the haze. On past the local version of the DVLA, bombed by the Maoists a few years ago and putting in McMillan windows. If the PIRA went into TUAS (Totally Unarmed Strategy) in 1996, then the Maoists are in NUAS (not using arms strategy...just at the moment) but the war carries on by other means. The latest campaign is to oust the coalition government with a Marxist Leninist Prime Minister, presumably because he's not left wing enough. They also are increasing pressure through advocacy of Federal initiatives. If what held Northern Ireland together was a strong centralised state structure (unlike Lebanon etc), then Nepal, with its already weak state structure, is being beckoned to further chaos and instability. No doubt the Maoist para state structure would then helpfully step in to restore 'order.' They perhaps have overlooked the fact that federalism may mean more power for groups advocating unity with India (the regional Great Satan).

I reach a school behind solid iron gates, with security guard. It's the Einstein Academy. You don't have to be a genius to get in there, but I suppose it helps. As I take a picture, someone taps my elbow and asks, "What is your name?" She's an immaculately uniformed, charming young girl of 14 or 15. I reply and answer other questions as to why I'm visiting Nepal, if I like it etc...

I turn the questions back round to school with, "What's your favourite subject?"

She looks at me quizzically. "English", she replies but her eyes complete the sentence with, "of course, you insulting fool".

"Do you like it here?"

"No", she thoughtfully replies, "Too many people and too much dust." "Where do you want to live then?"

"London", she replies, after a little thought..."to be an accountant."

I ask her name. "Priyanka", she replies. It's 7am and the bell goes. She rushes in through the step, through door in the thick metal gate, which closes with the security guard stepping through straight after her. For Priyanka, another day on the road out begins, and ten metres away, a man scavenges through a rotten pile of rubbish by the side of the road for reusable debris. That's the contrast of this place - privileged learning and escape routes next to the most basic expression of recycling. I turn round and begin to walk back to the flat. I've photographed enough misery and think it's all been summed up by Priyanka and the rubbish man by the side of the road. A Bono lyric comes to mind: 'Take these shoes, click clacking down some dead end street...and make them fit.' I walk for 40 minutes, on past the correct turn off and get lost...again.

At 11 am, we visit Asha Bal Bikash Sewa (ABBS) which is inside the new Human Development Community Services (HDCS) headquarters. It's the Babooshka of the acronyms visit. HDCS is a Nepali Christian NGO, active in areas of health care, community development and education and training. Their building was kitted out a couple of years ago via, amongst others, a grant from FONIC Trust. They manage 3 rural hospitals, in remote and therefore poor areas, as well as run health clinics and provide support for the so called untouchables. They surveyed two Wards in Rukum district (Mid-West Nepal) and found 500 disabled children (remember Lato?) so they set up a regional support fund and ABBS which provides day care facilities and promotes inclusion for up to 50 young people with severe learning and/or physical disabilities.in Kathmandu now runs a support programme for families of disabled children in Rukum.

We meet Mark Gill here again. From an Anglican Church in Greenisland and sent by CMS Ireland, he keeps bumping into us. You'd think he'd know his way around as he's been here since 1983. He initially worked in Hydro Power, then community development. More recently, when he's not colliding with people, he only oversees all HDCS construction projects, like this massive new building and a couple of hospitals here... and there. He's off to there in a couple of weeks, to the remote west of Dadeldhura, to rebuild a new hospital, section by section, round the old one, and also for fun, to put up an accommodation block and training facility! It'll take 2 and a half to 3 years and could have lots of spin off potential for new schools and facilities. He doesn't get up to that much!

Organisations like HDCS have real credibility with the Nepali government in the provision of quality health and community care. The opening doors to Christian NGO's are then another arena within

94

which people can have real impact on communities. Deborah worked with them for a number of years as a Nurse Educator at Lamjung Hospital while also co-ordinating medical electives (placements for medical trainees). CMS Ireland partner with and financially support HDCS across the range of its work.

Before I arrived, Philip had carried out a 1400 km trip for Mahema into the west. And after I leave, the plan is that they will both go 150kms south to visit Lalghat Leprosy Hospital, which will be part of the Mahema orbit. I learn that leprosy, if caught in time, can be successfully treated. The older forms of leprosy (with whole hands/digits missing) have diminished greatly because of much more effective village screening programmes. I just wanted to check that he wouldn't be slacking.

Last afternoon and even though I have limited right to permit it, a bit of tiredness has set in, so a lazy afternoon with some packing ensues. It's nearly 30C outside. Perhaps the monsoon will start earlier than July this year, when the sticky dripping heat slows all. I hook up my iProd but then I realise I need the cultural balance of an iMick! But they were all taken back to Dublin with the Samaritans Purse Team last year. Darn!

Suddenly it's 5pm and we're setting off for the chaos of the centre, with a bit of tourist shopping in the Thamel district. We pass fleets of Maoist buses returning from a rally and head for a final meal in Kilroy's Irish Bar and Restaurant. Owned by Bob, a low key but gregarious Canadian entrepreneur, he came to Kathmandu in the 1980's, liked it, met Kilroy, the chef and hence cooked up one of the best restaurants in Kathmandu. Vegetarian starters are followed by a mix of chicken and nax cheese (female yak cheese), Irish stew and fish with chips in a newspaper cone. Everest beer and a flaming candle birthday cake, delivered by line of singing staff, take the embarrassment of ageing birthdays into a whole new arena. The background hum of a generator that kicked in at 7pm is the white noise of a meal out in Kathmandu.

Out through the teeming side streets, rooftop bars restaurants and clubs, past the dance bars of the Soho end of town and the street kids. We pile into the Isuzu and negotiate a 20 point turn aided by ticket attendant and opposed by screaming taxi driver. We head back in total darkness through the centre of the city with, as usual, the only lights being from the shop fronts and the other traffic.

Just as in daylight, no one slows or alters their driving protocol of might is right and total individualism, where, if I can nip across or round you and you have to stop to avoid me, so be it! What I'd really like to avoid though, is the pungent aroma that slices through the nasal area as we approach and cross the Bhagmati River, rivalling the slurry pit of your nightmares. Adaptability and resilience are obviously essential criteria if one were to consider working in the Third World. I'd add to the desirable criteria, the possession of a very, very weak sense of smell.

Commiserations but see another 2 days of bonus features. It's a bit like: first prize is a Daniel O'Donnell album, second prize is two albums.

Day 13

Departures/ Delays/ Doha/ The Buffet/
Nothing on the TV

5:50am on the ring road to the airport, an elephant trundles ahead of us. I don't think he's wearing a mask! I am deposited by Philip and Deborah and I want to keep farewells as brief as possible. It's been an absolute privilege, I say and mean it. We bow and exchange Jai Mashi's (Christian greeting in place of namaste which means 'victory to the Lord') and see you laters.

I'm sitting in Kathmandu Airport reflecting and digesting all that has happened. A bit more of U2 morphs into: take this pen, scribbling down some dead end street ...and make it write.

Flight's delayed by 5 hours. I'll miss the connection in Doha for London but will hopefully get the next one and spend a night in London before heading finally home. I arrive in Doha only to be told that the next flight will be in the morning ...to Frankfurt and then onto Belfast at 4pm. I remonstrate and say I need to get home ...don't want to spend the night here... get me on the next flight to London etc. "It's full", the man claims, "and Frankfurt is the next fastest connection". I leave, then return to remonstrate with various airline staff. The fact that a 5 star hotel is offered doesn't impress. Doha: land of summits, dripping with wealth and sun, sea and er...sand.

There wasn't much Shalom around though as a group of five Israelis grasp the full horror of an afternoon and night in Doha, before being shipped round the Gulf tomorrow to arrive in Tel Aviv a day late. I foolishly decide to offer sympathy and engage in tag team remonstrations to airline staff in a pleading, "Get me to London" requests. No doubt they were thinking, "Get thee to ....". With a range of passers by looking on in an unfriendly way, I withdraw from the British-Israelite alliance in a resigned but dignified way and ask about transport to the hotel. Standing outside in 30C, topping up the tan until I wilt, I decide that the pickup bus is an Arabian mirage and get a taxi to the Movenpick Hotel instead. The taxi provides slightly more substance. Five Star and up on the 23rd floor, style wins over vertigo!

I fiddle with all the 37 lighting combinations and then endure a 5 star shower. Altitude sickness kicks in but I endure it with fortitude to sink onto the largest whitest softest bed in the world, emerging two hours later to shuffle to the lift and the buffet. A very tall fleshy African man in the lift eyes me with suspicion and asks brusquely, "Where are you from?"

Thinking this is a security person alarmed at how this specimen in non designer crumpled clothes has infiltrated the building, I select the Irish option and return his question. "Sudan", he says, in softer tones. "Lots of fighting there", and I think our little Anglo Irish War was a mere skirmish by comparison. I empathise, "Much better here". He nods and we exit at Buffet floor, with collar unfelt. Too many options, too little time so I decisively choose a mix of Egg Curry, Cashew Nut Curry, Chicken Biryani and Mekhani. Not overly helpful, digestively speaking! I reassure myself that it won't affect a slightly loose bowel syndrome. Perhaps I made a slight error there!

I check out the channels and get the latest from Qatar, Bahrain and UAE Sports I and 2. The commentary is ecstatic over a match that wouldn't get onto the lowlights of the Unibond League. I switch to Vietnam TV to catch up and a Mekong Delta Village (people) musical fails to live up to its billing. There's nothing on! Bed.

Day 14

Doha/ Munich/ Budapest/ London and Belfast (It's better to arrive than to travel hopefully)/ The Green.

The morning brings a rising orb over the marina opposite and I bus it to the airport at 6am, past the shining towers of affluence and blue overalled African workers enjoying a kick around at an under construction road to somewhere important. Perhaps their children will watch the World Cup here in Qatar in 2022. In the land of your exile, you've got to have some benefits. At the airport, more Chelsea shirts are evident; the mark of a new Roman empire.

I board the bus for the Frankfurt flight, past these lines of grey and white giants, in almost combat fatigue grey. Engines idling and fans turning, they await permission to climb above all else. I examine the faces in the bus; the usual mix of nationalities but the man next to me looks uncomfortably like Andreas Baader in his prime. This sets off a brief recall of Bernhard Schlink's musings on the crises of post war identity, however, this Kinderexpress only has a little North African ringletted girl on the housing and her baby brother on his back happily awaiting evacuation to Germany. Fine people I nod, with Lufthansa waiting to complete the rescue effort, for a stranded Ulsterman, winging him back to Belfast.

I get to Frankfurt, exit and ask for directions to the Belfast flight, only to be told by baffled staff that there is none ...but there's a flight to Budapest at the given time. "That's very kind of you, but perhaps on another occasion"! German efficiency sets me on a flight to London Heathrow and my connection to Belfast City, arriving exactly 24 hours later than booked for. I step off the plane, to be told my bags have been sent to Birmingham! I revise the German efficiency stereotype. The cool Belfast air, the sheer luminous green of the countryside on our drive back to Bangor via smooth wide roads, with impeccably manicured verges and centre sections, the so few cars and such restrained driving, all come as such a very pleasant calm to

the senses, that I want to get out and kiss this Northern Irish ground.
The circle's turned.

Conspiracy of Hope:

July 2010

Contrasts/ Behind Enemy Lines/ The Weather/ Conspiracy of
Hope/ Boring Bangor/ the People/ Loaves and
Fishes/ First to Last

How do you dare to define a trip into such a land of contrasts and the
range of people who pour out their lives because they just have to?
Inadequately of course, but I mentioned earlier the best analogy I
could come up with - a sort of wartime one, that they were, in a way
working and resisting behind enemy lines, disrupting chaos with
pockets of order, laying down payments through a Conspiracy of
Hope, all towards a different kind of future.

In true whistle stop fashion, I did get some (only some) snapshots, a
little of the flavour of the place, as well as the range of projects
FONIC and others are engaged in, through these western eyes. So
how did a soft westerner cope? Well, surprisingly well, if you do
things at your own pace. You see, there isn't any need to hurry there
and it's best to breathe it all in, rather than breeze along the trails.
The summer would be an ideal time to visit again, but it's monsoon
as I write this in early July. July and August have an average of 21
wet days each month and a rather alarming 88% humidity. Round
Pokhara is the wettest place in Asia, which means it's even damper
than Fermanagh. So it's March/April and October/November that
provide the best opportunities and the most clement weather
conditions, with temperatures in the mid 20's Celsius.

It would be great to get to ABC (Annapurna Base Camp); that would
be an achievement! I'm told it could be trekked up to in three days,

moving from Nayapul, to Ghandruk and thence straight north or, there's the possibility of just jumping on the single engine prop from Pokhara up to Jomson, flying over the Annapurnas and walking back down, taking it in a kind of flanking manoeuvre. Anyhow, the mountains sort of stay with you, in this place of often intentional and proud difference which even extends to the possession of its own time zone, set at five and three quarters hours ahead of GMT whereas everyone else is on the hour or half hour. I'd go back there yesterday...but that deal's not available just yet.

Looking at FONIC up close and the projects and people they support, one can see the real advantage of having people on the ground who can respond flexibly to need and operate outside a traditional mission organisation, spanning the expatriate community and the Nepali churches and groupings. They have the facility to network well and build lasting relationships, spotting new leaders like Abraham Khan and getting behind them, encouraging from inside the GCC/Business as Mission tent and doing the hard work of establishing an ethical trading business.

What became clear was that this daily investment of time and energy was for the long term. The McMillans' decision to spend it this way has produced its own ironic payoffs and consequent disadvantages: Nepal is home, it's got into their bones and they're just a little bit lost back in Northern Ireland. Furlough means exile. The last couple of days there provided the explanation for this: driving round, in and out and past the markets; the bustle; the meetings; the bumping into colleagues and acquaintances; the hive and drive of activity; the sense of purpose and difference made. I then began to understand what lay behind Philip's sudden question, "Do you see why we find Bangor a bit boring?"

And as for the Nepali lifestyle: people with so much less but living intensely and communally on every street - a sort of exaggerated version of the kind of extended family living patterns experienced in many of the little urban villages and enclaves dotted around the

101

Belfast of the recent past, where everyone knew your name and your Granny or Auntie could watch out for you or tell you off and send you back to your own street.

Many do live intensely, as it could indeed be a short life, caught between fate and hope. They say it's the hope that kills you but that's just not true. It's the hope that makes it possible to bear the grinding activity required for mere subsistence. They may be in a precarious position, but they also possess an innate resilience given the odds stacked against them by: their terms of trade, their location, plus the endemic instability and lack of good governance.

The wonder is that this country holds together at all. Perhaps it's because the chaos is a shared chaos. Their daily stock is the tests that come to us thankfully only occasionally, as when during the Troubles, people in Northern Ireland adapted by scaling down their expectations and just getting on with things, whilst a chaos too large to comprehend, never mind control, swept the tumbleweed through abandoned city streets and quietened towns - a hint of stoic Blitz spirit.

The glaringly obvious lack of economic and political infrastructure means Nepal can only present its people as its most valuable and valued resource. Their negotiating position is weak though; unattractive as they are to the external investment sources so badly needed. As a consequence, they can only sweep up the crumbs falling from globalisation's adjoining tables, spread out in India and China. However, development, even in hollow form continues apace, with the rural poor increasingly abandoning the villages, feeding a rapid urbanisation that creates all the supply crises that planning authorities cannot properly meet. They are drawn, as we all would be, by the promise of a better future, only too often to fall and keep on falling in the absence of the only partial safety net that there is here: family.

So, in dance bars, streets, remote villages and camps, a whole swathe of people do what can be done, bringing small loaves or fishes and seeing if they can be multiplied or stretched even further. Still others, scattered in unassuming and unmarked expatriate embassies representing the highest authority, make calls back home for further resources - resources that will encourage or enable the individuals, family groups, congregations or micro businesses who are compelled by an outrageous hope, which requires the last word in this war of the worlds. This hope then is transmitted through: the binding up of wounds, lifting up with care and prayer and relentlessly working to accomplish change by pressing in there even closer, bridging some of the distance between what is and the way it should be.

This country's long march into the morning continues apace, and in that confused, contradictory and uphill journey, some of the very best of our own are walking with them, taking towels and washing feet, all because of a belief that one day, last will be first.

 Meet the Yak, a particular hardy breed found in the high altitude regions of Nepal. A female Yak is called a Nak.

Steam Distillation! As promised..........................

The steam distillation process is literally sketched out on a white board for me. Fire heats up the water, which cause steam to rise. The raw materials such as Lemongrass or Chamomile are placed into the chamber and the natural oil fixes onto the steam; the steamy oil mix goes down the pipe to condense round rods. It then turns into a liquid of wateroil (the cold makes the oil and water condense and in the condenser they separate). The oil rises to the upper half and water is below. The oil drops into another compartment where the oil literally can be run off via a tap into a can and the remaining water goes back into the water tank of the distiller and can be made more efficient by heating via solar panels to raise the water temperature at the commencement of the process...like.

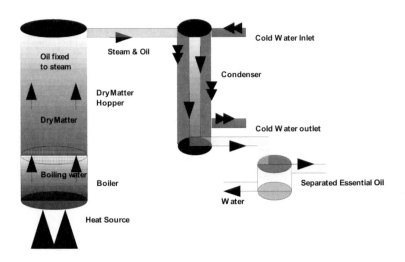

You'll find out more information on places and organisations mentioned by checking out the following websites:

FONIC Trust:	www.fonictrust.org
Mahema industries:	www.mahemanepal.org
Clanrye Trading:	www.nofatcats.com
	www.clanryetrading.com
	www.essentialoils4sale.com
GCC-Nepal:	www.gccnepal.com
Top of the World	
Coffee:	www.topoftheworldcoffee.com
International Nepal Fellowship:	www.inf.org
United Mission to Nepal:	www.umn.org.np
Human Development	
Community Services:	www.hdcsnepal.org
HCJB	www.hcjb.org
Kathmandu International	
Congregation:	www.kiccnepal.org
Higher Ground Enterprises:	www.facebook.com/.../Higher-Ground-
Beauty for Ashes:	www.facebook.com/.../Beauty-for-Ashes/
CMSIreland:	www.cmsireland.org
Kilroys:	www.kilroygroup.com
Sacred Valley:	www.sacredvalleyinn.com
Moondance:	www.travbuddy.com/Moondance
Womens Skills	
Development	www.wsdp.org.np
Samaritan's Purse	
Ire / Team Hope	www.teamhope.ie
Purchase goods made in Nepal	www.aunepal.co.uk

105

Support FONIC Trust

The profits generated from the sale of this book will be channelled to FONIC Trust to assist the work it does in support if the Nepali Christian Community.

FONIC Trust is a recognised charity in the United Kingdom. Its work is wholly dependent on charitable contributions.

If you would like to support FONIC Trust there are several options available to you.

1. Make a one-of contribution using Paypal via the FONIC Trust website www,fonictrust.org/donation.

2. Give to FONIC Trust on a regular basis monthly/ quarterly/ annually by completing the Bank Standing Order Mandate on the reverse page.

3. If you are a UK taxpayer increase your contribution by completing the Gift Aid mandate overleaf.

4. Consider including a contribution from the residue of your estate to FONIC Trust in you Will. A conversation with your legal advisor can arrange this. We would be grateful if you informed us if you commit to supporting FONIC Trust in this manner.

5. Why not encourage your friends, youth group, church or business colleagues to arrange a fundraising event. For fundraising ideas and a particular projects please contact the Administrator via email at info@fonictrust.org

If you are resident outside of the United Kingdom arrangements can be made with partner organisations to enable you to give in a tax efficient manner.

If you don't want to cut out the next couple of pages yet you still want to support FONIC Trust please email **info@fonictrust.org** and ask for Standing Order and Gift Ad mandates to be sent to you.

STANDING ORDER MANDATE

To the Manager of _____ Bank plc

Address_____

_____ Post code _____ Sort code   -   -

Please pay the First Trust Bank, 85 Main Street, Bangor, Branch

93 - 82 - 03 to the credit of: FONIC Trust A/C No 06285031

£figures.........   _____

................words......   _____ ....

on first payment   /   /...and thereafter every month/quarter/year*

until further notice/until last payment* / /____

(Note * - Delete as appropriate)

from Account No_____ _

In the Name of Capitals incl. Title_____

Signed   Date   /   /

Note to the bank from account holder [Please tick if appropriate]

☐   This is a new Standing Order mandate

☐   This replaces my Standing Order for £   payable to

_____ .

Join our Legacy Group
leave a donation to
FONIC Trust
in your
Will.

It's a common myth that only the rich and famous leave money to charity when they die. This couldn't be further from the truth. The reality is without gifts left in Wills by people like you, many of the charities we know and support today wouldn't exist. Whether it be a bequest of £50 or a percentage of the residue of your estate, a legacy of any kind makes a difference.

If you choose to bequeath a legacy to FONIC Trust in your Will, please ensure that you clearly state:

- the full and correct name of the charity
- the charity's address
- the recognised charity number

- Please request this information from the Trust Administrator by writing to **The Administrator, FONIC Trust, c/o P.O. Box 1144, Belfast, Co. Antrim, Northern Ireland.**

It is always recommended that you consult you solicitor when compiling or changing your will.

For we brought nothing into the world

and we certainly can't carry anything out. !

(I Timothy 6:7)

GIFT AID DECLARATION

Name: _____

Address: _____

_____

Postcode: _____

In accordance with Inland Revenue guidelines, please treat all donations I have made to FONIC Trust in the last 6 years and all donations hereafter as Gift Aid donations, until I notify you otherwise.

NB: For the tax to be reclaimed on your gift, you must pay an amount of Income Tax and/or Capital Gains Tax equal to the tax we reclaim on your donations.

Signature: _____   Date: _/_/_.

Please send this form to:

> The Administrator
>
> FONIC Trust
>
> c/o P.O. Box 1144
>
> Belfast
>
> Co. Antrim   Northern Ireland